Cross-Examination

The Evidence for Belief

Subodh K. Pandit, M.D.

CAMPUS p.r.e.s.s.

Publication, Resources, and Educational Services for Students
Ann Arbor, Michigan

P.O. Box 2402
Ann Arbor, MI 48106, USA
info@campus-press.org
Printed in the United States of America

Cover design by John Yoon
Editing by Ken McFarland and Thando Malambo
Layout by Ken McFarland

Revised and expanded from the original title, *Come Search With Me: Let's Look for God,* Copyright © 2008 and 2009 by Subodh K. Pandit, M.D.

Unless otherwise indicated, Bible quotations are from the New King James Version. Copyright © 1982 by Thomas Nelson Inc., Nashville, TN.

The Quran references are from *The Koran With Parallel Arabic Text.* Copyright © 2000. Translated by N. J. Dawood. Penguin Books.

Bhagavad-Gita references are from *The Bhagavad-Gita. As It Is,* by A. C. Bhaktivedanta Swami Prabhupada. Copyright © 1986 by Bhaktivedanta Book Trust.

Chapters 15 and 16 of Section Two are primarily based on pages 285 to 328 and 3 to 16, respectively, of *The New Evidence That Demands a Verdict* (NEDV), Josh McDowell, Nashville TN: Thomas Nelson, 1999.

Pandit, Subodh K.
Cross-Examination: The Evidence for Belief / Subodh K. Pandit, M.D.
1. Apologetics 2. World Religions 3. Philosophy of faith 4. Christianity
I. Title

ISBN: 1-890014-13-3
ISBN: 978-1-890014-13-1

CONTENTS

Dedication

Section One:

To Mary Pandit

Words will not begin to tell how much you mean to me. Your constancy and love have guided me through life. You are the one person in whom are embodied the qualities I admire and cherish most.

Ma, it is an honor and a great joy to dedicate this section to you.

Section Two:

To Maloti Pandit and Parul Ortiz

This section was written while wading in deep, dismal floods of pain, rejection, and loneliness sweeping in from many fronts at once. Maloti (whom we laid to rest on October 16, 2009 in Toronto, Canada, and whose loss has left me heavy, with my tears unassuaged) and Parul were like pillars made of angel-stuff, whose constant support and encouragement saw me through those trying days. With deep gratitude I dedicate this section to my two caring, wonderful sisters.

From the Publishers

Is your religion true because you believe it, OR do you believe your religion because it is true?

Some have argued that belief is neither rational nor coherent; that it does not need to be affirmed by evidence of any kind. Others stubbornly hold on to beliefs that blatantly contradict common sense, while validating their illogical stance with the cry of, "This is what **I** believe!"—as if belief in something renders it truth. If this assertion is valid, one can believe just about anything.

Yet belief that does not rest on solid evidence is little short of mere speculation. Belief does not absolve one of the responsibility for rational thought and careful examination of the evidence. One doesn't just believe, one believes *in* something. Faith in the irrational is nonsensical; it would be better not to believe than to have such a faith.

It is for this reason that CAMPUS p.r.e.s.s. is delighted to introduce the book in your hands. The fruit of one man's search for convincing evidences for belief, it will challenge you to step out of your comfort zone and master the courage to weigh the evidence. We encourage you to read it with an inquiring and honest mind. It may leave you no farther than it found you. But it just may lead you *to* truth. It's a risk, but one that we think is well worth taking because *blind* faith is just that: blind.

The Publishers.

Preface

I was born and brought up in India, a land with a rich and varied cultural heritage that goes back to 3000 B.C., to the Indus Valley Civilization—one of the oldest-known civilizations in history. The epochs contained in fifty centuries of cultural, political, religious, and military upheavals have made India what it is in this day and age. Today, it is a land teeming with a vast population of over a billion, who live amidst an amazing diversity of language, culture, food, dress, and religion. A few hours' journey by train can take you from a spot of familiarity to one that seems like a different country altogether.

India has the largest Hindu population in the world. The number of Muslims is the second largest of any country and surpasses that in most Muslim countries themselves. Buddhism was born, cradled, and nurtured there. It flourished in the eastern regions before spreading to the whole of Southeast Asia. Tradition has it that Christianity was brought to the peninsula by St. Thomas, one of Jesus' own disciples. It arrived there, then, in its earliest nascent form. Sikhism and Jainism have their roots in that soil.

What a crucible of mixture! What an environment in which to grow up! With shoulders rubbing in day-to-day encounters, questions naturally sprang up in my mind and were, at times, very troubling.

Yes, I did ask questions—many questions. So let me take you on a journey of inquiry.

My journey.

It began innocuously—just mulling over the way people made religious claims. But once I decided to evaluate it for myself, it became a gripping adventure. For one thing, like the others, I too had made claims and had felt rather good about them. That is, till I did some honest introspection, when suddenly, those claims did not seem all that convincing. The gap between the talk and the actual evidence was too big for comfort. There was a great deal of high-sounding religious jargon but little else. I sensed that void and knew I had to address it. My challenging yet exciting journey had begun.

The first questions I faced were deeply puzzling. I wanted to brush them aside and go on to more exciting themes, but try as I might, I just could not bypass them. They were the simple, broad ones regarding life, religion, and God that have been around for millennia and yet seem fresh to every generation. "What was life all about? Was there an ultimate purpose to it? How could anyone talk about a God they had never even seen? Did this God have an identity—maybe a name?"

Through the next twenty years I unobtrusively questioned as many people as I could and was amazed at the variety of answers I got. From the elite to the coarse; from the humble and hopeful to the proud and pretentious; from the blindly believing to the scornfully skeptical; the spectrum was wide indeed. Where and how was I to start the sifting process? Standing before such a myriad of voices, unable to decide whether to listen to just one voice or the whole array, was a distressing dilemma.

More than that, my burning issue and what I really craved was solace. I longed for a safe, sturdy foundation on which to stand when the going got tough and I desperately needed explanations. For when those haunting questions began their relentless pounding, my meager knowledge was no match to withstand them. The answers did not become satisfactory just because they came from those I held in high esteem. Conviction, it seemed, could not be passed on passively, either through the genes or as a contagion. I would have to struggle with each question myself. That foundation, to be stable and meaningful, would have to be personally and painstakingly laid.

But was a foundation to be found? What if there was no such thing? Well then, I wanted to know that for myself. And if there was one, I felt compelled to find it.

I started out and soon realized that just a cursory glance—a half-hearted attempt, arbitrarily picking up a point here or there—would not do. I would have to be open to the full weight of evidence.

If I was afraid of being proved wrong and even more afraid of having to make changes in my life, my quest was doomed even before it had begun. Of course, being open and fair under such circumstances was easier said than done, yet I could not make that an excuse for not trying.

So I made a choice—to start where the ground was level, taking the place of a common person "on the street" and facing the myriad voices without wearing my "emperor's clothes." The dilemma notwithstanding, I felt I had made a beginning. But would I remain fair throughout? This thought was always troubling, even though I knew that nobody on earth had risen completely free of bias and intolerance. I would just have to take it as a challenge and do my best.

So now let's get on with this journey. If I prove to be an unworthy companion, the solution is simple—just drop the book.

But if you agree that "give and take" is integral to community life, that respect and honesty can peacefully coexist, and that differing views need not spawn rancor or hostility, I invite you to keep company with me. After all, how pleasant and enjoyable can a journey be without fellow travelers and companions!

Section I

The Search

Introduction

Every journey has unique features, and if we look out for these attention-grabbers, the fascination they produce will hold up the interest the whole way. So watch for them—I think there will be enough to keep us from snoozing!

But first, we need to prepare ourselves with two crucial preliminary exercises:

1. Introspection
2. Proper Atmosphere

Introspection

Why do we need to examine ourselves? Because, unconsciously, we bring along a cartload of notions and ideas that can impede or divert us. Built up over the years, they cannot be rooted out easily, even when the stakes are high. How many peace talks between the Palestinians and the Israelis have broken down because of hatred and suspicion, handed down from previous generations, which they had unwittingly harbored? Centuries after declaring, "All men are equal," people still cannot shake off their ingrained sense of superiority. We are prone to go by preset values that we are unwilling to change.

We need to be careful about one particular attitude—pride in claiming to be open-minded. We like to be known as reasonable, balanced individuals. But we are seldom fair and unbiased. And here's where introspection is vital. We all have, blended in us, the mind of a *believer*, a *skeptic*, and an *inquirer* and can flit from one to the other so smoothly that we ourselves don't notice the change. The problem surfaces when we go straight to the believing or skeptical mode without going through the process of inquiry (all too common on the religious front). Then, when we are closely questioned or taunted regarding the basis of our beliefs, it comes as a shock that we cannot defend what we had taken for granted all along. We become confused and begin to question our own positions. This leads to greater confusion, because the answers are not easily forthcoming. This vicious cycle can get so frustrating that some feel great relief in turning their backs on anything that has to do with religion. I can sympathize with that. If you are in such a state, let me assure you that you are not alone.

Some shelve their frustrations, pretending everything is OK. Others silently wonder from whence the right answers are going to come or if they will ever come! But take heart, all is not lost. To those who question and grope, our SEARCH will make the most sense and be the most rewarding.

I had mentioned three attitudes inherent in us. Let us try to describe them. Here are seven sets of statements to consider:

One

Skeptic—decides against a claim prior to thorough investigation

Believer—decides to accept a claim prior to thorough investigation

Inquirer—withholds a verdict till investigation is done

Two

Skeptic—prefers those questions which introduce doubt

Believer—prefers those questions which establish as fact

Inquirer—asks questions mainly to gather information

Three

Skeptic—focuses on the questions, to the exclusion of the evidence

Believer—focuses on the evidence, to the exclusion of the questions

Inquirer—focuses on the weight of evidence

Four

Skeptic—disbelieves in the face of reasonable evidence

Believer—believes in the face of big questions

Inquirer—accepts reasonable evidence, even if some questions remain

Five

Skeptic—won't believe unless there is infallible proof

Believer—doesn't need any rational explanation for belief

Inquirer—willing to be swayed but only by evidence

Six

Skeptic—unwilling to make counter-proposal—it might be disproved, too

Believer—unwilling to make a counter-proposal—no need for it

Inquirer—willing to evaluate both proposal and counter-proposal

Seven

Skeptic—height of intellectual attainment is to ask, not expecting an answer

Believer—height of faith is to remain unshakable, no matter what

Inquirer—seeking a position of height not yet attained

During our sojourn, let us choose the attitude of an inquirer—one who withholds a verdict till the investigation is done. The believing and skeptical attitudes are so subtle that it will take frequent reminders to remain an inquirer throughout. But our first job is to make the choice.

Proper Atmosphere

Numerous attempts to scale Mt. Everest (at 29,028 ft., the highest mountain peak in the world) had to be abandoned. The swinging, unpredictable atmospheric conditions such as wind, temperature, ice, visibility, etc. would suddenly become mean and menacing, forcing the climbers to turn back and give up in frustration—another attempt aborted, despite all the meticulous and expensive preparations. It might have been different if the surrounding conditions had not become so harsh and hostile.

Fortunately, for our journey, the conditions are not entirely out of our control. We can choose and maintain the atmosphere that will surround us. But to create such an atmosphere, we will need the following: (1) Humility, (2) Honesty, (3) Calmness, and (4) Respect. We must pave our road with them, taking care to see that none is overlooked or discarded, because the absence of even one will severely hamper us.

1. Humility

This is of utmost importance and is irreplaceable. All other factors are secondary to it. Some tend to think of it negatively, as a groveling, self-depreciating posture; but humility is not concerned about a public image and is not something put on. Rather, it springs up and grows as we contemplate the vastness, beauty, and grandeur of truth. Even without defining it, we know from deep within that truth is unimaginably great and awe-inspiring. All who have reflected on it have been compelled to a sense of sacredness and reverence. How small we feel in its presence! And *that* forms the true basis of humility.

We can also realize truth on a lesser scale, as we appreciate the wealth of knowledge in those around us. Humility effectively leads away from pride and arrogance to an attitude of learning. The mind is mellowed to become open and accepting.

Nothing can be as important as humility in our search.

2. Honesty

This is a scarce commodity! I've met with all kinds of cover-ups, pretenses, and "white lies." People will do anything, just to avoid the appearance of ignorance. I've also come across a peculiar notion which holds that if we are strongly convinced about something, our enthusiasm and passion should be accepted as sufficient evidence of its validity. An impartial inquiry is not required, and honesty can be put aside, so long as we are defending what we feel honor-bound to defend. This has become so much a part of us that it will take more than an ordinary effort to recognize and reject it. One way is to make a definition of honesty that is sharp, clear, with "teeth" in it—and then rigorously apply it. Here is such a definition: "Honesty is the willingness to accept and acknowledge the value of a point or argument, no matter who brings it to the table, even if that affirmation has the possibility of destroying my own previous stand." I call this the "Wow Factor." If a point or piece of information is impressive, we should be willing to let it amaze us. We should be willing to say, "Wow!" and mean it, rather than first considering the implications and acknowledging only what is "safe"—only that which will support our positions and beliefs—but that would be unfair. We should be prepared to go where the evidence leads.

To inquire seriously is to inquire honestly.

3. Calmness

Back in 1879 after more than a thousand experiments, Thomas Alva Edison finally succeeded in inventing and producing the electric bulb. The challenge had been to find the right balance between heat and light in the delicate filament inside. In scores of experiments, either the filament would not glow sufficiently, or just when it did, it got too hot and burned off the contact points.

Religious discussions also require a balance. They can get dull and stereotyped and end in complete apathy, or become so vitriolic and bitter that broken relationships, enmity, and even war result.

Calmness is keeping our volatile emotions in check because we recognize it to be in line with humility and honesty. We make this choice so that the matter at hand can be evaluated fairly. If we are not humble and honest, emotions are bound to get out of hand, and once they do, they instantly dominate and sever the contact with reason and judgment. Conclusions will be anything but correct and fair; whereas, if we stay calm and balanced, the contact will be preserved. Light, meaning wisdom and understanding, will have a chance to glow. Calmness ensures that the light stays on.

4. Respect

Many think that respect automatically implies agreement. It does not. In fact, it shines out best when there is disagreement. We also tend to use it as a synonym for admiration. But this is not necessarily so.

We respect when we allow the other person whatever rights we claim for ourselves. Whatever freedom we use in making our choices, we freely grant to others—even if their choices are totally against our personal values. Mutual respect means that we, ourselves, are granted that same freedom by others.

Respect will never allow us to look down our noses at those who differ from us and call them names, hurl insulting epithets, slip in damaging insinuations, or condescendingly pity them. To be able to respectfully disagree is a virtue and will, in turn, bring respect even from critics and antagonists. Respect will bring credibility to our findings.

Humility, honesty, calmness, and respect form a strong foundation. But how do we make a practical application? The first step is to join the person "on the street"—one who has no loyalty to any particular religion or philosophy.

During the seminars I present, we go through a little ritual to symbolize this. The attendees stand up, draw an imaginary circle around their feet, and then step out of that circle, signifying letting go of those philosophies. Of course, it is only a ritual. Nobody can abandon deep-seated ideas in just a moment. The meaning is not to discard them altogether but to refrain from rising up in passionate defense of them. Our inclination to pride, dishonesty, and emotional outbursts will lose its grip on us, because what we wanted to defend has been laid aside. We now have no bone to pick, no ax to grind. The freedom this brings is *vital* to a search such as ours.

Let us accept and genuinely desire to implement these virtues, and they will provide the atmosphere that will take us the distance. No guarantees—just the best chance.

1

The Existence of God

"Allah ho Akbar," proclaims the Muslim cleric from the highest minaret of his mosque, sending those words to the farthest corners of his community. "Allah" is the proper name of God in Arabic. "Ho Akbar" means "is great." What he really means to say is that Allah is greater than any other. With these words he exhorts the faithful, at the appointed hour, to "salat" (prayer), one of the five fundamental pillars of the Islamic faith.

"Shema Israel," intones the Jewish rabbi, with a *kippur* on his head and the *tallic* (ceremonial shawl) around his shoulders. He is in the presence of the sacred Torah, the Books of Law in which are recorded the words that Moses received directly from Jehovah on Mt. Sinai. "Adonai Elohenu, Adonai achhod." ("Hear O Israel, the Lord our God, the Lord is one").

"Om mani padme hum," recites the Tibetan Buddhist monk, while his Japanese counterpart repeats, "Namo Amitabh, Namo Amitabh." The Tibetan's mantra is one of the most sacred: "O the jewel in the Lotus." The Japanese chants the "Name of Amitabh," a *bodhisatva* (one who has reached the penultimate state—just before attaining Buddhahood), who presides over the Pure Land Paradise.

"There is no other name under heaven," thunders the Christian preacher/pastor, "given among men by which we must be saved." The name he refers to is Jesus of Nazareth, the son of Mary, who was called the "Christ," meaning the Anointed One, the Messiah. He was also called "Immanuel," which means "God with us."

Deep in the Indian peninsula, a guru and his *shishya's* (followers/students), saffron-robed and with shaved heads, break into a chant while on a pilgrimage, "Hare Rama, Hare Rama, Rama, Rama, Hare, Hare. Hare Krishna, Hare Krishna, Krishna, Krishna, Hare, Hare." Rama is the seventh *avatar* (incarnation) and Krishna the eighth, of the God Vishnu, the Preserver of the universe.

Widespread and diverse—this religious world!

On the other side of the fence stands the rank skeptic, the avowed atheist. With a wry smile on his face, he condescendingly taunts, "Oh, these poor, deluded souls. How utterly futile to sip at 'the opium of the masses'!"

For that is what Karl Marx had called religion. He felt that those who believed in religion and God were using them just as props and crutches to hobble through life, hoping to deaden the sense of pain and suffering which formed the reality of life. And what was more, this life was utterly purposeless. All claims of heaven and a utopia somewhere out there had been brought in because of the inability to face the naked truth of our present aimless existence. There was no God, no after-life, and no heaven. Nobody knew where we came from or where we were going.

Was this the "reality" that everyone else had missed? Bertrand Russell, a brilliant, British atheistic philosopher, in an essay (*Why I Am Not a Christian,* 1957, p. 106), giving his reason for refusing to become a believer, said that it is **"only on the firm foundation of unyielding despair that the soul's habitation can henceforth be safely built."** I immediately felt the clash of ideas in that sentence. For how could "despair" form a firm foundation; how could "unyielding despair" ever be "safe"?

Quentin Smith, another atheist, and co-author of *Theism, Atheism and The Big Bang Cosmology,* was blunt:

> **"... The only reasonable belief is that we came from nothing, by nothing and for nothing."** (Oxford: Clarendon Press, 1995), p. 135.

And what was such a bold, sweeping claim based on? The only reasonable answer I could come to was, *"Nothing!"* This was as wild a guess as any I had ever come across. If the base was "nothing," it could uphold nothing, and Russell's "unyielding despair" probably was founded in nothingness. But nothingness or emptiness is not an easy philosophy by which to live. It is a hard, unrewarding principle. No wonder Jean-Paul Sartre, the French thinker and philosopher, after waxing eloquent on his well-structured arguments for discarding the notion of the supernatural and God, confessed that the only question that remained was why he had not committed suicide! Albert Camus, a Nobel Laureate, concluded:

> **"The final philosophical question is the question of suicide."** *The Myth of Sisyphus and Other Essays* (New York: Vintage, 1955), p. 40.

The "nothingness" of Smith will force one toward the "unyielding despair" of Russell and ultimately drag the soul to the precipice of Sartre and Camus. Such is the depth to which these despairing philosophies and questions can drive us.

But just because somebody was despairing and wanted to commit suicide did not make it wrong. I knew of religious and pious people who also wanted to commit suicide. Merely shooting out labels and libels at one side or the other would not do. The underlying question had not yet been answered—the question of whether or not God existed. This had to be faced squarely first. What was the use of looking for a named river or lake, if the existence of water itself was in question?

Does a God Exist?

To this question, there can be only two answers. The response of those who say they do not know and cannot decide is not an answer. Such a response could be a confession of ignorance on their part or a claim regarding paucity of knowledge on the subject, but it is not an answer to the question.

The two answers are:

A) God is non-existent; fictitious.
B) God exists and IS, in fact.

The claims are irreconcilable and mutually exclusive. I call it the Great Divide.

"The universe we observe has *precisely* the properties we should expect if there is, at bottom, no design, no purpose, no evil and no good, nothing but blind, pitiless indifference." Richard Dawkins, Oxford Biologist in Science, in *River Out of Eden* (New York: Basic Books, 1995), p. 133.

"... The seemingly arbitrary and unrelated constants in physics have one strange thing in common—these are *precisely* the values you need if you want to have a universe capable of producing life.

... There is no good reason for an intelligent person to embrace the illusion of atheism or agnosticism." Patrick Glynn, in *God: The Evidence* (Rocklin, CA: Prima Publishing, 1997).

Notice how both the statements use the word *precisely*, claiming to refer to "facts" that they say are freely available. Something had to have gone awry, if both were referring to facts and yet making diametrically opposing and mutually exclusive claims.

One factor, I think, is the way the debate is structured. Each side makes claims for itself and then challenges the other to disprove them or make better claims. The drawback to this type of thinking is the tendency to come to conclusions by default: If I showed good evidence for my side, then by default, the other side could not—or on the other hand, if I showed the other side's claim to be deficient, then by default, mine was established. But on looking over the scene, I found that there was enough support for each side to stake their claims and few enough deficiencies to keep either side from making dogmatic, silly (meaning unsubstantiated) statements. I have heard believers mockingly describe apes and monkeys as the ancestors of unbelievers, without realizing that it would apply to them, too. I have read atheists who propound the "scientific law" of evolution, without giving a second thought as to whether the word *law* would stand scrutiny. Neither of these is true, and neither statement impressed me. I wanted the "facts" so that I could make up my own mind.

So, I drew up what I called the Pan Process, which I hoped would keep me in the mode of inquiry. When there are two mutually exclusive options, the tendency is to build two columns of arguments: one showing the positive points for your side, and the other showing the negative points of the opposing side. This is good as a defense for what one has already established, but the Pan Process, a process of inquiry, requires four columns—two columns for each option—one for (pro) and one against (con).

Once the four columns are filled, we can step back and see if the weight of evidence tilts the balance one way or the other.

"Pan" stands for:

1. Going across boundaries, scanning the whole horizon, as in the ***Pan***-American Games.
2. The process of sifting, like a person who ***pans*** for gold, separating the valuable from the ordinary.
3. The first three letters of my family name, ***Pan***dit.

The Pan Process

Proposal A—God is non-existent; fictitious.

Column One: Arguments for Option A

There are none! Surprised? But it's true. This is because the statement is a negative one. A negative statement is valid when, and *only when*, all the possibilities have been exhausted. If I claimed that there were 10,000 lakes in the USA and none of them was named *Char gog agog munchaug agog chau bun agun gamuag,** how many lakes would I have to be familiar with? All 10,000. Even 9,999 will not be sufficient to establish that claim.

Let's apply this to just one factor regarding God, His location. He could be residing anywhere in the universe. None of us can claim to know every nook of the town in which we live, much less the country, or the world, or the moon, or the solar system, or the Milky Way galaxy with its one hundred billion stars, or the one hundred and twenty-five billion galaxies estimated by the astronomers. By what stretch of imagination can a human claim to be familiar with all that! And it isn't as if we've looked at most of the places and only a few now remain to be checked out; rather, what we do know compared to what is unknown is so little as to be counted closer to zero than any number. Even if we had checked

*Note: There is such a lake in Massachusetts. It is the longest name in the U.S.A. and is in the Native American language. Translated, it says, "I fish on my side of the lake, you fish on your side, and nobody fishes in between!"

out 99 percent of the universe, we would still have more than one billion galaxies left to inspect!

Furthermore, this God could probably move about. If you went looking for Him in Canada, He could have gone to India. To make a valid claim then, we should know every spot in the universe and be everywhere at the same time. This is called omniscience and omnipresence. They are the characteristics attributable only to God. So, to exhaust all the possibilities and thus prove that there is no God in existence, one has to possess the attributes of God or become a God himself! The tangled knot is evident. There are no arguments in this column.

Column Two: Arguments Against Option B

I believe there are four such arguments.

1. Lack of empirical evidence
2. Presence of pain, suffering, and cruelty
3. Lack of design, or the presence of bad design
4. Difficulty with "creation"

1. Lack of Empirical Evidence

Empirical evidence is a direct form of knowledge, such as seeing, touching, and tasting for yourself. I have never seen or heard God, as I do other humans. This confession could imply that there is no God. But I have also never seen or felt so many other entities or realities, yet have believed in their existence, such as my own brain, or the chemical formula for water. They constitute reality to me and to everyone else I know. The majority of scientific deductions fall into this category. I do agree with the observation that many who say that they have heard God cannot provide evidence for it. So yes, empirical evidence is missing, and that could be an argument but perhaps not the strongest one.

2. Presence of Pain, Suffering, and Cruelty

This is a fairly strong argument, because of the claim that God is good and kind. Darwin struggled in trying to reconcile the idea of a good God with the cruelty he saw in nature. However, thinking closely, it is not an argument against the existence of God but against the *kind* of God being described. In other words, if some of these questions were satisfactorily answered, and He was found to be good and kind after all, He could very well be in existence; on the other hand, He just could be a bad God but in existence all the same.

Another question also arises. Pain and suffering do not constitute the whole spectrum of our experiences. Exquisite pleasures and deep joys are also to be found. If pain and suffering point to the absence of God, what do such joys and pleasures indicate? To be fair, they should point to the existence of God, so at best, these observations nullify each other. This is obviously not a simple problem but a huge, crucial one. Consequently, I took a closer look at the claims. (See page 196, Appendix A, for my discussion on it.)

3. Lack of Design or Presence of Bad Design

First, the argument need not refer to non-existence but rather to something not done adequately or in the right manner by this God. It could actually be a subtle confession of His existence.

Second, designs are all around us—myriads of them. Not simple ones such as a wooden toy car but designs that are complex, intricate, and extremely precise. Yes, some areas appear chaotic and disorderly, but if these suggest the absence of God, then to what do the millions of mind-boggling designs point? A broken vase is still a vase. To point only to the jagged, broken edge and claim complete lack of design in the whole structure is false reasoning.

Chaos in one area does not change design at another point to anything other than design. If there is both design and randomness in the same structure, it is the design that takes precedence and provides the correct feature of that structure, even if present in small measure. But design is not present in just small measure in nature. Rather it is overwhelming in its extent. What appears to be lack of design and bad design shrinks into insignificance in the face of the magnitude and precision of design all around us. It would be unscientific and untruthful to ignore this.

4. Difficulty With Creation

I faced two problems when trying to explain creation. One, it is not something that has been observed. Two, it is not in conformity to any known law of nature or science.

Thus, to the rational mind which invariably seeks an explanation, to simply claim that it happened in a particular manner is not at all satisfying. *Creatio ex nihilo* (creating something out of nothing) does not appeal to reason. The dependence on belief/faith is obvious and has to be conceded. But if this is not acceptable, is there another explanation that is superior, in which scientific evidence and logic take the place of this take-it-or-leave-it type of story? Will a completely random, totally undirected, unsupervised event such as the Big Bang of Singularity fit the bill? More on this later.

In the Newtonian type of approach, appealing to a known law would have been a strong argument. But after the questions raised by quantum physics and the relativity of Einsteinian thinking, we know we are at a loss to explain, let alone enunciate, a law regarding all we observe. Therefore something outside of our present repertoire of knowledge need not be the basis for making final conclusions regarding such huge, all-encompassing ideas as the presence or absence of God.

Proposal B—God exists and IS, in fact.

Column Three: Arguments for Option B

1. Circumstantial Evidence
2. Logical Analysis
3. The Anthropic Principle
4. Instant Formation of Granite

1. Circumstantial Evidence

▸ Sheer Numbers

If just one person told me that there was a calf with a head attached to both ends of the body, I would easily dismiss the report. If 500 people testified to it, I might not believe it right away, but I would give it a second thought. If a million said the same thing, my response would shift from disbelief to considering that there could be a good possibility that such an outlandish creature did really exist.

Billions believe in the existence of God and are willing to testify to that from personal experience. Shifting from disbelief to the possibility of truth to the claim is therefore reasonable.

▸ Deep in Human Psyche

From the dawn of human history, there has never been a single generation that did not believe in the existence of the supernatural. If an idea has stayed around for a century, it should lend a measure of credibility to it. If it persists for thousands of years in the hearts of millions and billions in an unbroken chain till today, it becomes a form of evidence that is difficult to disregard.

▸ Presence of Design

Every scientific discovery, whether in the subatomic sphere or in the gigantic world of astrophysics, has shown in greater and yet greater force the overwhelming presence of design in the very structure of nature and the universe.

Why is it that we never hear of an archeologist (an acknowledged scientist) who unearths an ornate pillar from the rubble and then declares, "It happened by itself. Nobody made it. I never saw the one who could have done it"? Why was he able to differentiate it from the dirt around it? Because there was design in the pillar and none that was obvious in the dirt. Now, what if there is design in the matter that makes up dirt? Shouldn't a scientist acknowledge that and go looking for the maker of that matter, just as he went looking for the maker of the pillar?

Why would a jury not accept a story from a defendant who described a gun coming out of its case from the closet and turning and firing at the victim "all by itself"? Nobody saw the person who did it!

The most die-hard skeptic will not accept such ideas. They will be dismissed even before they are stated. Why? Because a design or a purposeful act demands the presence of a person, a mind, behind it.

All the manufacturing units in the world put together would not equal the complexity, intricacy, and precision of even one system such as the nervous system in our bodies. Multiple systems are in us, multiplied numbers in the animal and plant world and in the universe, all working together with an uncanny coordination. True, it is not proof of the existence of God, but it is powerful evidence of a mind out there. Why would anyone propose the idea that these vast systems happen all by themselves?

2. *Logical Analysis*

- **The Kalam Argument. Al Ghazali, a Muslim who lived in the eleventh century, formed a simple three-step deduction:**

Step one: Anything that begins has a cause.

Step two: This universe has a beginning.

Step three: Therefore, the universe has to have a cause.

- **The "Pan" Argument. Three steps are stated again:**

Step one: "Scientists" claim that matter, energy, space, and time are the only entities in the universe. Nothing else exists. Nothing is supernatural.

Step two: The cause of a substance or product lies outside and is transcendent to the substance/product. For instance, the wooden table cannot be the cause of the wooden table, nor can we say that wood is the cause of that table. The carpenter could be the cause, but he is distinct from the substance/product.

Step three: Therefore, we cannot appeal to matter, energy, etc. as the cause of matter, energy, etc. The cause must be distinct from the substance. The Cause has to be supernatural.

This Cause must possess at least two characteristics that should conform to what we observe in nature. First, material nature in the vast universe of 125 billion galaxies is complex and intricate to an overwhelming degree. The Cause, therefore, can be deduced to possess an ability of immense proportions—a giant intellect able to conceive, execute, and keep tabs on the whole multifaceted structure. Albert Einstein described his **"rapturous amazement at the harmony of natural law, which reveals an intelligence of such superiority that, compared with it, all the systematic thinking and acting of human beings is an utterly insignificant reflection."** Mircea Eliade, ed. *The Encyclopedia of Religion (*New York: Macmillan, 1995), p. 322.

Second, the energy involved in the universe is of a magnitude beyond our comprehension. The cause must at least match that magnitude of power inherently, so as to provide energy for the mightiest cluster of galaxies on the one hand and be able to control it sufficiently to focus on a subatomic particle, on the other.

A giant intellect possessing immense energy could refer to something like God. Nothing precludes such a conclusion.

3. Anthropic Principle

This term was coined in 1973 by British scientist Brandon Carter and describes the factors that probably started and maintain life on Planet Earth.

These factors are so many and so precise that a spontaneous, random cause is extremely unlikely.

> **"Take the expansion rate of the universe which is fine-tuned to one part in a trillion, trillion, trillion, trillion, trillion, trillion. That is, if it were changed by *one part* in either direction—a little faster, a little slower—we could not have a universe that would be capable of supporting life."** Stephen Meyer, a philosopher whose field of study was the history of molecular biology, the history of physics, and evolutionary theory, as well as "origin of life" biology, quoted in Lee Strobel, *The Case for a Creator* (Grand Rapids, MI: Zondervan, 2004), p. 78.

> **"Gravity has an incomprehensibly narrow range for life to exist"** (Robin Collins, a physicist, mathematician, author, and philosopher who studied under the legendary Alvin Platinga, quoted in Strobel, *The Case for a Creator*, p. 132).

> **"When you combine the two, [gravity and cosmological constant] the fine-tuning would be to a precision of one part in a hundred million trillion, trillion, trillion, trillion, trillion, trillion. That would be the equivalent of *one atom* in the entire known universe!"** (Collins, *Ibid.*).

"...The original phase-space volume required fine tuning to an accuracy of one part in ten billion multiplied by itself one hundred and twenty-three times ... would require more zeros than the number of elementary particles in the entire universe!" (Roger Penrose, in *The Emperor's Mind,* quoted in Strobel, *The Case for a Creator,* p. 135).

Let's look at another factor—our location in space:

"It is only in the inner edge of the Circumstellar Habitable Zone where you can have low enough carbon dioxide and high enough oxygen to sustain complex animal life. And that's where we are" (Guillermo Gonzalez, astronomer, physicist, and co-author of *Privileged Planet,* quoted in Strobel, *The Case for a Creator,* p. 174).

"We happen to be situated safely between the Sagittarius and Perseus spiral arms.... I really can't come up with an example of another place in the galaxy that is as friendly to life as our location" (Gonzalez, quoted in Strobel, *The Case for a Creator,* pp. 169, 171).

And we have not even scratched the surface of the number of factors of this kind. (Examples: The sun being the right mass with the right ratio of colored light, the right composition, the right distance, the right orbit, the right galaxy, and the right location; the structure of the solar system, with specific features of our moon and of the planets, the earth itself, with its location, size, composition, atmosphere, temperature, internal dynamics, and many intricate cycles such as the carbon cycle, oxygen cycle, nitrogen cycle, phosphorus cycle, sulfur cycle, calcium cycle, etcetera—all to nurture living organisms on a circling planet.)

"Over the past thirty years or so, scientists have discovered that just about everything about the basic structure of the universe is balanced on a razor's edge for life to exist" (Collins, quoted in Strobel, *The Case for a Creator,* p. 131).

Another consideration is regarding the fact that we, on Planet Earth, are peculiarly positioned to make scientific observations. Ours is probably the only location in the universe from which a total solar eclipse can be viewed and experienced. This has allowed scientific studies of the color spectrum of the sun which would not have been possible otherwise. It has helped establish the only observable part of the Theory of Relativity, which states that gravity can bend light. It also provides a historical record of changes in the earth's rotation. The sun is 400 times the size of the moon and is exactly 400 times the distance. The area they occupy in the sky is exactly equal, one to the other. **"It's that**

incredible coincidence that creates a perfect match" (Gonzalez, quoted in Strobel, *The Case for a Creator*, p. 185).

> **"Our location away from the galaxy's center and in the flat plane of the disc provides us with a particularly privileged vantage point for observing both nearby and distant stars"** (Gonzalez, quoted in Strobel, *The Case for a Creator*, p. 187).

"The very composition of our atmosphere gives it transparency" (Jay Richards, philosopher and theologian, co-author of *Privileged Planet*, quoted in Strobel, *The Case for a Creator*, p. 188).

> **"To find that we have a universe where the very places where we find observers are also the very best over-all places for observing—*that's* surprising. I see design ... in this very pattern of habitability and measurability"** (Jay Richards, quoted in Strobel, *The Case for a Creator*, p. 189).

This would be like going to the control room at the Kennedy Space Center just before a final countdown and finding every one of the hundreds and thousands of dials at exactly the precise point necessary for the success of the whole venture—from the initial planning to the safe return of the space shuttle—and then claiming that it all happened by sheer coincidence! Yet even this illustration pales in comparison with what we observe in nature. To place every one of the thousands of needles at the only point on each dial so as to originate and perpetuate life requires a master control center. To me, any other explanation would be far inferior to this and leave more questions unanswered.

4. Instant Formation of Granite

Granite is said to be the primordial rock of the earth, formed over geological time scales of multiplied millions of years. The elements then present were subjected to certain ranges of temperatures and pressure, to gradually synthesize the rocks that we see all over the world today. But discoveries from the famous Oak Ridge Laboratory in Tennessee, U.S.A., which were published in standard and prestigious international scientific journals, tell a completely different story.

Polonium 218 (Po-218) is a radio isotope without an earlier form (precursor) and has a known half life of three minutes. The radiation causes a signature halo in the particles of rock during the decay of the isotope. Any substance, then, that has captured a halo, had to do it in three minutes or less.

It has been incontrovertibly demonstrated that granite rocks from around the world, including the gigantic El Capitan and Half Dome Rock in Yosemite National Park, California, contain Polonium 218 halos in such quantity as to establish the widespread nature of the phenomenon. The scientific deduction is astounding—those giant rocks, that seem to make up the foundation and framework of the crust of Planet Earth, were formed in three minutes! See *Creation's Tiny Mystery,* by Dr. Robert Gentry (or go to www.halos.com on the Internet).

Nobody has yet formed a piece of granite in the laboratory using the theorized raw materials and the temperatures and pressures proposed—suggesting that such a theory should be open to question. Nobody has yet demonstrated an original fossil embedded in granite rock—suggesting that no extended period of time was involved in the process.

I met Dr. Gentry personally, in April 2008, in Maryland, and in August 2010, in Florida, U.S.A., where he clearly stated that nobody had yet successfully challenged [disproved] these significant findings.

Therefore, until such time as they are shown to be false, we have no option but to accept the present scientific conclusion that the event—formation of granite—most likely took place in three minutes, and not over millions and millions of years. The personal opinions of bigwigs in scientific circles cannot make this more or less than a scientific fact, based on the best evidence to date.

As inquirers, we should rely on evidence, not on opinions and unfounded theories. However wrong the "three-minute" claim may ultimately turn out to be, the scientific inquirer inside us should not bow to any but the best available, reasonably established information of today.

Column Four: Arguments Against Option A

Statistical Analysis

"Chance" is a subjective idea that we all use every day in making a host of decisions—and is also a mathematical tool called probability. The relevant numbers are plugged into a formula, and the result gives us an indication as to whether an event might or might not occur.

In day-to-day life we can say that an event that has only one chance of occurrence in 10^8 (100 million) is considered an impossibility, and 10^8 chances of occurrences to one of non-occurrence as fact. In scientific evaluations the number goes up to 10^{15} (quadrillion). When it comes to stating a scientific law, we are told that the number is 10^{50}. In other words, if there is a mathematical probability of something occurring 10^{50} times, with only one chance of failure, the event is said to have been established as a law, meaning it will always occur. Conversely, if there is only one chance of occurrence and 10^{50} chances of failure, the event is considered to be utterly impossible.

Of course, these numbers are arbitrary, but they are too huge to question. How big are these numbers, anyway? Let me try to illustrate. Suppose I wanted to test gravity by dropping a ball from my hand once every second and looking for that one chance when it will not come down but will stay suspended or simply float away. To test it 10^{18} times, it will take me 15 billion years. That is the age of the universe, according to the Big Bang theory. If I wanted to test it 10^{20} times, it would take 1.5 trillion years—100 times the age of the entire universe! So 10^{50} is, admittedly, arbitrary but is an astronomical figure, too huge to question. One chance, then, in 10^{50} is stating an utter impossibility.

Dr. Michael Denton is considered one of the first to statistically challenge Darwin's idea of spontaneous generation of life. He looked at the simplest cell that could possibly live and function. What were the chances that 100 proteins (the smallest number required) could come together by sheer coincidence? His calculation showed a probability of one in 10^{2000}! Ralph Muncaster, *A Skeptic's Search for God* (Eugene, OR: Harvest House, 2002), p. 93.

Remember, 10^{50} is an impossibility. Now, let's just suppose there was a colossal mistake in the calculation and the real number should be smaller by a factor of 100 billion. That would be quite a blunder for a scientist to make, but let's just say he did. What is 10^{2000} divided by 100 billion? Precisely 10^{1989}. We've hardly made a dent in it! So it is futile to question these numbers with a skeptical attitude.

Ralph Muncaster, in his book just cited, *A Skeptic's Search for God*, states that the chances of getting 10,000 amino acids with left-sided links (which is absolutely necessary), and 100,000 nucleotides with right-sided links (again absolutely necessary) together in one cell, is one in $10^{33,113}$ (p. 98).

Harold Morowitz calculated the odds of a whole cell randomly assembling under the most ideal circumstances to be one in $10^{100,000,000,000}$ (100 hundred billion)! (Ibid., p. 93.)

How about a "WOW"! To just write the zeros down at one per second will take more than 3,170 years! And we have not computed the other factors in, such as the exact function of each molecule, division of that cell, increasing biological complexity, life from some unknown source injected into the organism, plant life, or animal life or human life with such abstract qualities as love, courage, and honesty, etc. If the list itself is endless, what would the combined chances be for all the components to come into existence and then come together spontaneously, by sheer coincidence? Statistically, an absolute impossibility!

And here's some logic attached to the numbers: If there are two mutually exclusive options (A) and (B), only one of which is correct, then,

if (A) is possible, so is (B);

if (A) becomes improbable, (B) becomes probable;

if (A) is shown to be impossible, (B) becomes fact!

For example, if I asked what the square root of 25 was and gave you two options, only one of which was right, then proposed 33 as the first option but refused to tell what the other was, which would you choose? The second, hidden option, of course! Because the square root of a whole number greater than 1 is always smaller than the number. The first option of 33, being greater than 25, cannot be the right one. This makes option two the right answer. Strangely and yet significantly, you don't even have to see the second one to make that choice. It will still be the correct one.

If the formation of that first cell was utterly impossible by random chance, reason demands that we accept the only other explanation—that it was a supervised process/event. Let's put the columns together.

God, non-existent

Column one: NO arguments

Column two: They raise questions but are not strong conclusions

God, factual

Column three: Circumstantial evidence, logical analysis, and the anthropic principle together form a fairly strong argument

Column four: Statistical Analysis—spontaneous generation statistically impossible.

It appeared a fair evaluation, and the weight of evidence was difficult to deny. The balance was tilted decisively.

> **". . . The absolutely overwhelming evidence points toward an intelligence behind life's creation."** Walter Bradley, Ph.D., professor at Texas A&M, in *The Mystery of Life's Origin* (Dallas, TX: Lewis and Stanley, 1992).

> **"Science you might say has discovered that our existence is infinitely improbable and hence a miracle"** (John Horgan, *New York Times*, Dec. 25, 2002).

Why do scientists continue to disbelieve in the existence of God? I cannot answer for all of them, but there appear to be factors other than scientific ones.

> **". . . They're not excited because they disagree with the science; it's**

because they see the extra-scientific implications . . . they don't like where it's leading" (Michael Behe, author of *Darwin's Black Box,* quoted in Strobel, *The Case for a Creator,* p. 215).

"For a fruitful debate we need to understand evolution's foundation. . . . We need to understand this because ultimately evolution is not about scientific details. Ultimately evolution is about God" (Cornelius Hunter, *Darwin's God* (Ada, MI: BrazosPress, 2001).

"Spontaneous generation was disproved one hundred years ago, but that leads us to only one other conclusion, that of supernatural creation. We cannot accept that on *philosophical* grounds; therefore we *choose* to believe the impossible: that life arose spontaneously by chance" (George Wald, *Scientific American,* May 1954, italics supplied).

Others have been rather forthright:

"I didn't want there to be a God, who would hold me responsible for my immoral lifestyle" (Lee Strobel [as an atheist], in *The Case for a Creator,* p. 29).

"I don't want there to be a God; I don't want the universe to be like that." Thomas Nagel, *The Last Word* (New York: Oxford University Press, 1997), p. 130.

How do evolutionary scientists describe the origins of the universe and life?

"Singularity has no 'around' around it. There is no space for it to occupy, no place for it to be.... There is no past for it to emerge from. And so, from nothing, our universe begins. In a single blinding pulse...the singularity assumes heavenly dimensions, space beyond conception.... So, what caused it?...some quality or thing, that introduced a measure of instability into the nothingness that was." Bill Bryson, in *A Short History of Nearly Everything* (New York: Broadway Books, 2003), pp. 10-13.

This is supposed to be a scientific explanation! What is the basis for such unfounded statements?

"The laws of physics do not exist in a singularity" (*National Geographic Encyclopedia of Space,* 2005, p. 93).

So Bryson was free to state what was not in line with natural scientific laws. And how did life start?

> **"It was a singularly hostile environment and yet somehow life got going. Some tiny bag of chemicals twitched and became animate. We were on our way"** (Bill Bryson, in *A Short History of Nearly Everything*).

Now, really, is this an explanation at all? How is this different from the "difficulty with Creation" we had faced earlier? Nobody has ever observed this, and it does not conform to any known scientific law.

In the words of Henry Gee, chief science writer for *Nature* (1999): **It is "an assertion that carries the same validity as a *bedtime story*—amusing, perhaps even instructive, but not scientific**" (quoted in Jonathan Wells, *Icons of Evolution* (Washington, D.C.: Regnery Publishing, 2002), p. 221.

Misia Landau, author of *Narratives of Human Evolution*, was struck by the similarity between accounts of human evolution and *old-fashioned folk tales* (quoted in Wells, *Icons of Evolution*, p. 222).

> **". . . The materialistic views of Darwin, Huxley, Simpson, Monod, and Dawkins are based on personal philosophy, not empirical evidence . . . this is not science but myth"** (Wells, *Icons of Evolution*, p. 228).

Paul Davies from the University of Adelaide, Australia, is said to have stated that it is **". . . almost impossible for the non-scientist to discriminate between the legitimately weird and the outright crackpot!"** (Paul Davies, in *Nature*).

It would not be reasonable or fair to heap scorn on the "naïve" faith of those who believe in the "magic" of creation and then propose a "magical" event, without even a magician being present! I wonder which requires more of this "naïve" faith. (See page 206, Appendix B, for my philosophical discussion on ultimate purposelessness.)

I agreed with a statement made (on another topic) by George Hanson: **"The difficulties of belief may be great; the absurdities of unbelief are greater."**

I chose to believe.

2

Truth, Relativism, Pluralism

Returning home in my van from work, I heard this question over the radio: "Is your religion true because you believe it, OR do you believe your religion because it is true?" That question gripped me, and I could not get it off my mind. At first, I was tempted to treat it like a party riddle that a slick answer would easily dismiss. But when I tried to answer the question, I realized how profound it really was. The more I thought about it, the more complex it appeared. I jotted down some ramifications to each side to help me clarify them. The first, I labeled as a belief-based religion, and the other, as truth (or evidence)-based.

If my religion was mainly belief-based, then:

1. Every religion on earth would have to be accepted as true, so long as somebody believed it. For that matter, every statement, even if diametrically opposed to another, would have to be acceptable.

2. I could create the characteristics of "God" by my belief. If I believed God to be very strong, only then would that be true. If I believed "God" to be harsh and inconsiderate, well then, He was just that kind of God.

3. Belief would have the power to create truth.

4. My faith would totter if I met an overwhelming problem, because I would know in the back of my mind that the "God" I had created by my fancy was not bigger than the problem that I now faced in real life.

If my religion was evidence-based, then:

1. Every religion/statement would not carry the same weight. I would have to study the merits and demerits of each and place them on different levels of credibility.

2. "God" would possess His own attributes, whether I believed them or not. I could acknowledge them, but I could not bestow any on Him.

3. Truth would create belief/faith (and not the other way around).

4. I would have to provide sufficient evidence as a basis for my belief.

This led me to the all-important question: Could I honestly say that my religion was evidence-based—that I had good reason for my belief? One day when I was alone at home, I thought it was time to address the question. I decided to play "court of law" in my living room. I was going to be the judge, the jury, the defendant, the defense counsel, and the prosecuting attorney. The oaths taken, the session began. Within ten minutes, the jury, along with the public, was laughing and nearly taunting the defense counsel—so pathetic was the case and the arguments being presented! Every further attempt only made it more ridiculous. I had not realized that I was in such a defenseless position.

I was devastated!

When I had recovered from the shock, I decided to go on a journey of inquiry to settle this question for myself. I would keep at it until I returned with a satisfactory answer or realized there was none to be found.

Truth-Relativism

Some say that truth is not knowable—that it is out there, but we cannot grasp it with sufficient certainty to feel comfortable about it. So all a person can say is, "This is my truth, and that is yours. Nobody can claim to know real truth."

Others are equally firm in their stand that truth is knowable. Absolute truth may be beyond us, but what we can know is objective enough to refer to as fact.

I had to grapple with these claims before continuing, because my journey would not be necessary if there was no chance of knowing the *truth* of the matter. What was this thing called "truth," anyway?

Multiple concepts and definitions exist—enough to make one reel. So I narrowed them down to fit my quest for the reality of God. Three basic ideas, historically, await consideration.

First is what is called Traditional Theism: The reference is to a sacred written code, such as the Quran of the Muslims, the Bhagavad Gita of the Hindus, or the Bible of the Christians. Only the privileged few, the priestly class, may enter its holy precincts and then come out to us common people to instruct us on the meaning of the written text and the application of those mysterious pages to our lives.

Second is Modernism (synonymous with scientific truth). A few centuries old now, this challenged the exclusive rights of the clergy and established the scientific method of approach to truth. Anyone, not just the priestly class, could know truth, but it had to come only through the proper steps of investigation. Theories, experiments, data collection, and analysis of that data resulting in a conclusion, were the steps to be followed. The conclusions alone could be accepted as truth—all else was suspect.

Third is Post-Modernism (synonymous with subjectivism and relativism). This rules the intellectual world of today. It dismisses the two earlier ones with a sweeping claim: "No such thing as truth exists. All statements are only relatively true and, therefore, also relatively false. Nobody can claim to establish a fact anywhere in the world."

Whew! If there ever was a potpourri of ideas! I decided to examine them all.

Traditional Theism: Looking throughout history, the first impression was one of disgust and horror. The inhumanely cruel crusades, the murderous, mind-jarring jihads, and the perfidious papal inquisitions were all repulsive. If this was what those writings about God instigated, I did not want it at all. I turned away in revulsion.

Modernism: The method appealed to me. It was open and objective. The attempt to be precise was impressive, the mathematical calculations often going to the fourth and fifth decimal places. But the big drawback was the complete absence of the search for God. In fact, the idea of the supernatural was ridiculed. The focus was elsewhere, and I could not see any likely change in the near future. I would have to leave it to another generation perhaps.

Relativism: This appeared broad and easy-going. "You have your truth; I have mine. I scratch your back; you scratch mine." But that was only the case until the question of absolute truth came up. Then it was a bitter fight, with no quarter given and no compromise possible. Even the definition of absolute truth pertaining only to our sphere of existence was not acceptable. (One such definition: Absolute truth is that which is valid for all people, at all times, at all places.) See page 218, Appendix C, for my examination of this concept. This was not even a philosophy but instead, a mere "mood," as Ravi Zacharias labeled it, in *Jesus Among Other Gods* (Nashville, TN: Word Publishing Group, 2000), p vii. It did not stand up to scrutiny.

At this point, I was in an awful intellectual bind. I had discarded all three concepts. But I would still have to make decisions throughout the day. What principles would govern those decisions? A basis was needed at every step. A vacuum was just not possible. I realized I had somehow reached a false conclusion. I would have to re-think this through.

To my great relief, I found a discrepancy that left a door of inquiry still open. In examining modernism and post-modernism, I had grappled with the substance of what they were claiming. I had tried to weigh the arguments for and against the claims. But with traditional theism, I had slid off that point, focusing on the nasty behavior of certain people. These, I had equated with the stuff—the substance of their claims. I was right in my evaluation of their behavior but wrong in connecting it to the claims of the religion.

Yes, bad behavior was present, but that was not all there was to it. I had met some exceptional, wonderful people too. They were generous, pleasant, purposeful, and selfless, and I had a deep sense of admiration for them. They had clearly been a blessing to the community in which they lived. When asked for the secret, they pointed to their religious beliefs. So here was traditional truth producing both torture, as well as tremendous good. We all know families in which one child grows to become accomplished and graceful, while another turns out totally different. How fair would it be to point only to the troublesome child and discredit the family? No, it would not be fair to focus on just one side and ignore the other. I decided to evaluate the *substance* of traditional truth (traditional theism).

Pluralism

I was not prepared for what I next faced. Even a cursory glance left me stunned. From the scanty claims of the Sumerians, the Mayans, the Egyptians, and the legendary writings of the ancient Chinese and the Indians, to the more structured writings of Zarathushtara (Zoroaster), Gautama Buddha, The Hindu Vedas, the Analects of Confucius, Lao Tzu's Taoism, the Old and New Testaments of the Bible, the Talmud, and the Quran, it was a bewildering array that left me shaken. Dismayed and despairing, I sat down to think again. I had hit a stone wall. Multiple lifetimes would not be enough to study them all. Painstakingly, I had come this far. Would it be finally futile?

Cautiously, I began to ask around. What did others think of this daunting spectrum? Gradually, two opposing camps came into view.

Camp one (exclusivism), in which each boldly claimed that his/hers was the only one correct way—"Mine!"

Camp two (pluralism), in which each said that all the religions were only different paths to the same, final destination.

Both camps could not be correct.

I decided to look at pluralism first. If that could be established, I need not be alarmed, because I was already on a safe path. My search would be only to get more information within my own belief system. I could spare myself the struggle of delving into a hazy, nebulous field looking for something that I did not even know existed. (See page 224, Appendix D, for the scrutiny.)

It did not stand up to my examination. The obstacles were insurmountable, and I had to discard it. The claims took different paths and were definitely aimed at different destinations.

I turned my attention to exclusivism. I had rejected pluralism with good reason but was, by no means, out of the woods yet, for here were multiple claims, each clamoring for the status of "The only way."

What were the options I would need to consider? There were three:

First, ALL are correct. This is absurd and illogical. It would be like saying there are multiple prime ministers in India or multiple presidents in the U.S. This was not a real option.

Second, ALL are wrong. This was not illogical—it did not go against reason. But there were two obstacles I could not get around.

For one, to say that anything was wrong was to imply that I knew what was right and could use that special knowledge as a yardstick. But nobody on earth has the position, the knowledge, or authority to make such a claim. I could not.

For another, if all were wrong, I would have to discard them all, because they had lied at a fundamental level and had left me no assurance regarding anything else uttered. Also, one core claim found among the religions was the existence of the supernatural. I would have to discard that concept, too. But I had already established it to a reasonable degree at the start of my search. I could not say they *all* were wrong.

Third, the only one left. Somewhere out there was one claim, and **only one,** that was legitimate. Only one was truly the **only one**. In other words, there was ONLY ONE WAY to truth. Even if I would never be able to identify it, the credibility of this statement would stand.

As it sunk in, I realized that it was a critical, pivotal point of my search. Everything that followed would have to be held to this concept. It would become the uncompromising reference point henceforth. This was frightening, too. What if I was not on that path? What if I failed to recognize it?

I pondered the significance of this crucial conclusion.

1. The conclusion was reached by a step-wise deduction from a "neutral" angle, and, therefore, was credible.
2. It refuted the concept of pluralism.
3. It did not allow the followers of these religions to toy around with pluralism. For example, if a Muslim espoused pluralism, he would first have to deny the *Shahda,* the claims of Allah, and the Islamic faith itself.
4. The "only way" claim was a fundamental one. If a religion could not establish itself as the "only way," it would lose its standing, because it had proffered a lie at a basic level. It would have relevance only at the points in which it agreed with the "only way."
5. This claim was the most powerful motivating statement that could be made, meant to beckon one and all to a particular fold. Each founder wanted the followers to take him seriously—to forsake every other path and stay loyal, no matter the cost.

6. The distance between the top and the rest did not matter. Winning by even the slimmest of margins would be enough. A thousandth of a second can separate the Olympic champion from all other contenders and relegate them to an "also-ran" status.

7. A more critical factor than being ahead was being different. If there were four red marbles and only one green, then the green would be the one. If all but one were traveling west, then east would be the right direction. If all were running and only one was walking, then walking was the correct way to compete.

Whatever the significance, the question now was how to do the comparison. What method would I use to compare apples and oranges? To just describe the different features and make a choice based on my likes and dislikes was not possible. That would not help, because each of us has our own set of likes and dislikes; however, there was one possible way out of this predicament.

If the apple was ripe, sweet, and fresh, while the orange was old, rotten, and full of worms, the choice would not be difficult to make, especially when I was hungry. Notice, however, that the comparison was not actually between the apple and the orange but between "freshness" and "rottenness." Yet it would be a very reasonable choice, about which nobody would seriously disagree. Once freshness was preferred, the apple became the automatic choice.

Similarly, I knew I could not directly compare the different tenets of beliefs and the various doctrines to decide which was superior. I had no set of criteria that was universally accepted as a reference point to which I could bring these religious features for a standardized study. I would have to find other features that would indirectly help me make a choice.

What follows are the results of using those features. I initially chose five of the world's great religions and made a comparison, asking ten questions of each of them and looking for responses from their writings or from sources friendly to them: **Hinduism, Islam, Christianity, Judaism,** and **Buddhism**. Three questions were to be addressed to the religion's writings and seven to their flesh-and-blood founders. I would try not to discredit or downplay any claim. I would simply lay them side-by-side and score them as fairly as possible.

The questions were such that anyone could look for the answers. It did not require a specific religious interpretation. I was looking for the *facts* on which the adherents had made their religious interpretations. The part relating to the interpretation is religious and constitutes the claims of that religion. The part relating to the "facts" is not religious by nature. I did not have to be a follower to accept it. It is to this point that I directed my questions.

The ten questions are as follows:

1. What type of literature is the writing?
2. Does the writing open itself to be challenged for authenticity?
3. What is a top feature of the writing?
4. What is the highest claim of the founder for himself?
5. What is the nature of the message/mission of the founder?
6. How does the life of the founder compare with his own teaching?
7. How does the length of ministry compare with the results?
8. What are the reports of the birth of the founder?
9. What were the circumstances at the death of the founder?
10. What was the post-death scene?

I wondered if anything decisive would come out of such a process. Yes, the evaluations were going to be subjective. I was free to give whatever score I thought best. Nobody was looking over my shoulders to see if I was playing it fair. But if I were not honest, I would be fooling only myself. To me, this was serious business, and too much was at stake to try to manipulate the outcome.

Of course, questions will remain. They may make my decisions look bad. But a bad decision could be a good one—if the alternative is worse! (Conversely, a good decision could be bad, if there was a better option.)

So, keep your seat belts fastened with **humility, honesty, calmness,** and **respect**. The landscape ahead looks exciting. It is going to be quite a journey!

3

Literature

The Principle of Verifiability suggests that if there were two conflicting claims which could not be assessed directly, but they did have indirect factors which could be evaluated, then the one attached to a verifiable factor gained in credibility.

For example, the location of dim stars has sometimes been predicted, even before they are visualized. This is done by observing the movements of nearby visible stars, resulting from the gravitational pull between the celestial bodies. Later, with better telescopes and viewing techniques, the star would come into actual view. Now, suppose Astronomer A predicted the location of a star to be below the belt of the constellation Orion, while Astronomer B said it was above the belt. Both agreed that it was not visible to the naked eye.

Astronomer A offered no other information except his "gut" feelings, which had served him well earlier, while Astronomer B produced the results of prolonged studies showing the movements of nearby stars. This information had been double-checked by others and found to be reliable. This verifiable portion made the claim of B more credible. The star was most probably above the belt.

Similarly, the concepts of truth and doctrines in the ancient sacred writings cannot be tested directly for value and authenticity. But they have been handed down to us in the context of narratives, which can be tested for their historical reliability. The point of contact between the supernatural (religious claims) and human beings has to be in the mundane world first—in the course of day-to-day human existence. Secular history is the fundamental record of that existence; therefore, religious claims should have a historical context to have merit. The more concrete the historical terms such as events, places, and dates, the more the likelihood of the attached abstract claims—such as the nature of God and truth—being the original, authentic message.

The ancient writings may be classified into four broad categories:

1. **Folk Tales:** These make no attempt to state a real/true story. In fact, it is accepted that the narrative is fictional. The main intent is to be interesting and bring out a lesson/moral.

2. **Legend:** A legend is probably based on a true story, but changes crept in over a period—exaggerations and embellishments growing to superhuman proportions and slipped in generations after the event, when there were no longer any eye-witnesses to challenge the change. The time period required is usually centuries.

3. **Myth:** These are so far back in history that imagination is accepted as

the main ingredient. The characters and stories are most probably not true. Bizarre and unnatural elements are emphasized in as colorful a description as possible. The time period is usually many centuries, and even millennia.

4. **Historical:** The attempt here is to state the story as it really was, with no significant additions and no core changes due to distortions or overstatements. The closer the formation and recording of the narrative to the time of the event, the greater the credibility.

Let us see how the writings fare.

A. **Hinduism:** The earliest writings are the Vedas, followed by the anthology, the Upanishads; then the Ramayana Epic, and last, the Mahabharata Epic, within which is found the Bhagavad-Gita.

"Lord Krishna first spoke Bhagavad-Gita to the Sun-god some 100's of millions of years ago" (Preface to *The Bhagavad-Gita As It Is*, p. xix). It was lost and then repeated at the Battle of Kurukshetra about fifty centuries ago. Such a distant past makes it impossible to verify the stories. Most scholars accept the mythological nature of the writings.

B. **Buddhism:** The next four statements, in chronological order, regarding Gautama Buddha, are from K. K. S. Chen, *Buddhism: The Light of Asia* (Hauppauge, NY: Barron's Educational Series, 1968), pp. 62–64.

- "Was he not born at Lumbini? . . . Did he not complete existence at Kusinara?" ". . . the Theravada looked upon the master as a human teacher."
- "Soon after the passing of the master a change began to set in."
- "At the beginning of the Christian era, the transcendental nature of the Buddha became more and more pronounced."
- "In one of the most important pieces of Mahayana literature there is not much of the man left in the Buddha. He is now an exalted being who has lived for countless ages in the past and will continue to live forever."

This covers a period of about one thousand years, during which there is a clear change regarding the nature of the Buddha from an ordinary human to a superhuman level.

C. **Judaism:** There are thirty-nine different books and over twenty authors, living at vastly different periods of history. I could not find a way to give one consistent classification to the whole set of writings.

D. **Islam:** The Quran was put together in writing by 652 C.E. (Common Era, same as A.D.)—within thirty years of the life of Muhammad. The earliest manuscripts were destroyed by one of the Caliphs (Uthman), such that only one version remained. So we cannot compare what we have today with what existed in the beginning. However, since the first one was within one generation, we should place it among the historical type of literature.

E. **Christianity:** The earliest written documents were the letters of Paul, some of which were written within ten years of the life of Jesus. He came into the movement later, compared to the disciples of Jesus, so the information was established orally even before that.

"The tomb, excavated by Jewish scholar/professor, E. L. Sukenik, was dated by means of coins found among the coffins to a period before 41 AD. The stone coffins are marked with crosses and remarkable inscriptions: 'Jesus is God,' and 'Jesus Ascended One.'" (Preface to It Is Written Study Bible edition of *The New King James Version*, Thomas Nelson, 1982, p. iv)

The legend of Buddha took 700 to 1,000 years to form. Ten years is simply not enough time for such a phenomenon to develop. In the case of Jesus, there appears to have been no gap between the formation of the story and the events from which it was culled. The Gospels themselves, though of later date, were all written in the lifetime of that generation.

"We can already say emphatically that there is no longer any solid basis for dating any book of the New Testament after about AD 80." Sir William Albright, one of the greatest archeologists in the world, *Recent Discoveries in Bible Lands* (New York, NY: Biblical Colloquium, 1955), p. 136.

The New Testament should be classified as an historical piece of literature. That does not mean it cannot be questioned. It only means it cannot be treated as a legendary or mythological story. It means that the questions have to be dealt with in terms of historical evidence—much as we would debate the circumstances around the 1963 death of the late President J. F. Kennedy in Dallas. Nobody takes JFK to be a mythological figure and doubts the crux of his biography, just because of those questions and the severe differences in the "authoritative" reports making the rounds, even today.

How does the New Testament compare with other ancient classics which are accepted as unquestionably historical the world over?

Caesar's *Gallic Wars* was written in 100 B.C., and the earliest copy is dated A.D. 900.

Herodotus' *History* was written in 400 B.C. The earliest copy is dated A.D. 1300.

Tacitus' *Annals* was written in A.D. 100, and the earliest copy is dated A.D. 1100.

Note the gaps—more than a thousand years! We have no idea whether what we have in our hands is really what the author wrote, yet they are accepted without question by the general public. After swallowing a thousand years, it would not be fair to question and cavil over less than ten years!

Another pointer used for determining how creditable we ought to regard the text, is counting the number of manuscripts that back the literature—the smaller the number, the easier for changes to be made in all of the copies. The greater the number of manuscript copies and the distance between the manuscript copies—both in terms of geographic location and in length of time between productions of manuscript copies—the more difficult to slip in the same changes in all the copies. *The Gallic Wars* is backed by ten manuscripts, Herodotus' *History* by eight, and Tacitus' *Annals* by twenty. Homer's *Iliad* is high up there, with an impressive 643 manuscripts. When it comes to the New Testament, it is far and away not only the leader but in a class by itself, with 5,664 Greek manuscripts! If the Latin, Ethiopic, Slavic, Armenian, and other versions are added, the total comes to an astounding 24,000 +! See Josh McDowell, *The New Evidence That Demands a Verdict* (Nashville, TN: Thomas Nelson, 1999), p. 34.

"In real terms the New Testament is easily the best attested ancient writing in terms of the sheer number of documents, the time span between the events and the document, and the variety of documents available to sustain or contradict it. There is nothing in ancient manuscript evidence to match such textual integrity..." Ravi Zacharias, *Can Man Live Without God?* (Dallas, TX: Word Publishing Group, 1994), p. 162.

"No other ancient book has anything like such early and plentiful testimony to its text, and no unbiased scholar would deny that the

text that has come down to us is substantially sound." Sir Frederic Kenyon, *The Bible and Modern Scholarship* (London: John Murray, 1948), p. 20.

"In the variety and fullness of evidence on which it rests, the text of the New Testament stands absolutely and unapproachably alone among ancient prose writings." (F. J. A. Hort, quoted in McDowell, *New Evidence*, p. 35.)

"To be skeptical of the resultant text of the New Testament books is to allow all of classical antiquity to slip into obscurity, for no document of the ancient period are as well- attested bibliographically as the New Testament." John W. Montgomery, *History and Christianity*, (Downers Grove, IL: InterVarsity Press, 1971), p. 29.

I've heard numerous jokes and taunts regarding the "miracles" in the Bible, because it is treated as mythological. Some maintain, it is to be swallowed with a pinch of salt, like the legends of yore, such as the *Nordic Tales* or the *Arabian Nights*. I suppose this is to be expected on just a superficial consideration, but when fairly and closely examined, the facts point to a different classification.

We should let the evidence speak for itself.

4

Challenge

Did the writings have any form of checkpoints? Were inquirers free to review and inspect these sources for themselves? Could a claim be examined for authenticity, or was testing and examination discouraged? Was I supposed to swallow the claims without question?

A. **Hinduism:** "... we have to accept it as it is; otherwise there **is no point in trying to understand the Bhagavad-Gita and its speaker, Lord Krishna"** (*Bhagavad-Gita As It Is*, Preface, p. xix.)

B. **Buddhism:** "... the genuine realization of the emptiness of **the phenomenal world is ... a direct intuition of the highest truth. Absolute truth ... is unconditional indeterminate and beyond thought and word." (**Chen, *Buddhism, The Light of Asia*, 1968, p. 76.)

   In both these religions, the real-life experience of the follower was supposed to be the authenticating feature. It appeared as a good, bold point which made a lot of sense. However, if there were many religions out there, how practical would it be to get into the experience of each before making a decision? Indeed, to get into the experience of any particular one required a choice. And what about clear warnings from different religions of awful consequences that would follow for those who chose any other path than the one outlined? Experience before choice, to me, was putting the cart before the horse. I wanted a reason that I could think through before I checked it out by experience.

C. **Islam: "If men and jinn combined to produce a book akin to this Quran, they would surely fail to produce its like, though they helped one another as best they could."** (The Quran, 17:88.) In other places the challenge is to produce ten chapters like the Quran (11:13), or even one chapter (10:38).

   Here is a stated challenge. But when I attempted to test it, four snags killed the attempt.

   - The challenge did not state which feature was to be equaled—whether it was to be the prose, poetry, rhythm, diction, philosophy, doctrine, beliefs, or descriptions of God, etc.
   - It did not define the method of comparison. How would a decision be made as to whether the Quran was better, equal, or worse?
   - Who would be the final judge regarding the comparison? Would it be an Imam, a Muslim Council, a neutral body, an international

committee, or an individual, such as me? By default, I felt that I should be the judge. If so, then I think there are other writings that can equal the Quran in one or more aspects—Omar Khayyam, Rabindranath Tagore, and Jallaluddin Rumi, to name a few. To me, these writings are too beautiful to be surpassed.

- To the orthodox Muslim, Arabic is the divine language of communication, and the Quran is considered authentic only in that language; hence, to equal the Quran, the writing should be only in the Arabic language. I'm sure millions of Muslims do not know one sentence of literary Arabic. What then of the rest of the world? I was definitely not included in this challenge. The test had lost its universal character.

A subjective, nebulous challenge, applicable to only a narrow segment of the world's population, is not a real challenge.

D. **Judeo-Christian: "'Present your case,' says the Lord . . . 'Let them bring forth and show us what will happen... declare to us things to come. Show the things that are to come hereafter, that we may know that you are gods.'"** (Isaiah 41:22, 23).

This challenge is called predictive prophecy, meaning that both the prediction and the actual occurrence could be verified and established as separate entities. This is an intriguing test, because it involves "time." We humans are totally unable to break through the barriers of time, except in imagination. We can guess what might happen later, depending on certain trends, but we cannot predict with certainty anything, say, a century or even a decade, before it happens. The test points to superhuman knowledge.

Here is an example of such a prophecy: The Bible, in Jeremiah 56:36, 37, stated, **"I will make her springs dry . . . Babylon shall become a heap . . . without an inhabitant."** At the time of this prediction, said to be about 595 B.C.E., Babylon was at its zenith. The walls—fully fortified, broad enough for two chariots to run side-by-side, and rising to heights of 200 feet—were considered impregnable. The food supply in the stores was sufficient to last for twenty years, making a mockery of anyone planning a siege. But it fell to Cyrus the Medo-Persian in one day. He conquered it by draining the river Euphrates, which ran under and across the city into aqueducts that his soldiers dug, then marching his army into the city on the riverbed, once the *"springs were dry."*

And today,

> **"Few words evoke as many images of ancient decadence, glory and prophetic doom as does 'Babylon.' Yet the actual place, 50 miles south of Baghdad—is flat, hot, *deserted*, dusty"** (*Smithsonian*, June 2003, p. 50, emphasis mine).

Babylon is still "without an inhabitant." You and I are witnesses to the fulfillment of this prophecy.

If I predicted that your son would have curly black hair—when everyone in the family had straight blond hair—that at the age of 4 he would read all the works of Shakespeare, at 12 would graduate from university with a professional degree, at 20 would win an Olympic gold medal in swimming, at 30 would be awarded the Nobel Prize in astrophysics, and if all of these predictions came true, I dare say you would follow me to the ends of the earth to find out what my next prediction was going to be.

Of course you would! It would be an astounding set of predictions, setting me apart as "out of this world." How many more true predictions would be needed to establish my credentials? I would be satisfied with a dozen, wouldn't you?

Scholars tell us that *600* predictions in the Old and New Testaments of the Bible have come to pass. Over 300 pertain to one individual—Jesus the Christ. Over two dozen were fulfilled during one weekend, and some of them were predicted more than *a thousand years* before the events. (See McDowell, *The New Evidence That Demands a Verdict,* and Ralph Muncaster, *A Skeptic's Search for God.*)

The Judeo-Christian challenge is open and clear; it can be investigated by any ordinary person willing to do it and be honest about it.

5

Top Feature

These religions have more than one great feature. I picked some at random, yet these are considered the top ones by many people. They are all exceptionally impressive.

1. **Islam:** The language of the Quran is often spoken about and praised to the skies. **"When they listen to it, they feel enveloped in a Divine dimension of sound."** Karen Armstrong, *Muhammad* (New York: HarperCollins Publishers, 1992), p. 49. Tradition has it that in 616 C.E. a certain Umar ibn Al- Khattab was angry with the new religion and went looking for Muhammad, to kill him. He was deflected from his purpose and sent back home, where, to his consternation, he found that the hated Quran was being read right under his own roof. He punched his sister in the face, and everyone fled, leaving the Quran on the ground. He picked it up and read the opening verses of chapter 20:

 "'How fine and noble is this speech,' he said wonderingly, and this Muslim was felled . . . by the beauty of the Quran which reached through his passionate hatred and prejudice to an inner receptivity that he had not been aware of." He now went looking for Muhammad to confess his instant conversion to the new religion. (Ibid., p. 128.)

 Other stories tell us of ordinary people, as well as kings and rulers, who were struck with the beauty of the language and accepted the religion and friendship of the Muslims, to the point of becoming staunch military allies.

 "In the Quran, Muhammad is often called the 'Ummi' prophet, the unlettered prophet." (Ibid., p. 88.) Muhammad could not read or write. Others wrote out the Quran for him or memorized what he was saying and kept the information bank growing. That is why the book is called the Quran, which means "The Recitation." Muslims claim this to be a great miracle and an attestation of its superhuman origin.

 The language of the Quran is amazing, exquisitely beautiful, and, possibly, supernatural.

2. **Hinduism: "Hindu sages gave to mankind one of the most sophisticated systems of philosophy ever devised."** (National Geographic, *Atlas of the World*, 1975), p. 119.

 Taken together, the *Vedas*, the *Upanishads*, the *Epics*, and other traditional writings, form a grand network of information. They contain a blend of religion, ethics, civil codes, medicine, mathematics, astronomy, and other natural sciences thousands of years old and which astonish us yet today, in the twenty-first century.

They, arguably, invented the concept of "zero," which can represent nothing—as well as the largest number imaginable. Without the decimal system, mathematics and science would come to a standstill.

The Ayurvedic system of medicine has ideas that Allopathy has not understood yet.

Divisions of time (called "kashta") go down to the hundred-millionth of a second. The only point where science uses such numbers is in describing the half-lives of sub-atomic radioisotopes, such as the mesons and baryons, which we have come to know about only recently.

Hindu philosophy and information is also amazing, deep, brilliant and, possibly, supernatural.

3. **Buddhism:** The literature is vast, detailed, and mysterious.

- **Vastness:** The "Pali" canon fills forty-five huge volumes. The Chinese scriptures consist of 100 volumes of 1,000 closely printed pages each, while the Tibetan extends to 325 volumes. That's a total of 470,000 pages, half of which are yet to be translated from the original languages!

- **Detail: "The Lord's body had thirty-two marks of a super-man, and was adorned with the eighty subsidiary characteristics. He was endowed with the eighteen special dharmas of a Buddha, mighty with the ten powers of a tathagata and in possession of the four grounds of self-confidence."** Edward Conze, *Buddhist Scriptures* (London: Penguin Books, 1959), p. 22.

  The monks were subject to 250 rules, if you were male, and 311 rules, if you were female.

  A common prayer for forgiveness went, **"I beg leave, I beg leave, I beg leave. May I be freed at all times from the four states of woe, the three scourges, the eight wrong circumstances, the five enemies, the four deficiencies, the five misfortunes and quickly attain the path . . ."** Quoted in Ravi Zacharias, *Jesus Among Other Gods* (Nashville, TN: Word Publishing Group, 2000), p. 90.

- **Mystery: "The bulk of this literature is couched in a deliberately mysterious language which would convey nothing to the average reader." For Example, "The realization that undifferentiated**

emptiness is the sole absolute truth. Nirvana is therefore that mental state in which one realizes that all things are really non-existent" (Chen, *Buddhism, the Light of Asia*, 1968, p. 72).

Buddhist scriptures are also amazing, awesome, and mysterious and, possibly, supernatural.

4. **Judeo-Christian:** The cross-references among the authors is unique.

For example, between the authors of the Old Testament: **"I, Daniel, understood by the books, the number of the years specified by the word of the Lord through Jeremiah the prophet"** (Daniel 9:2). Daniel is recommending Jeremiah.

Between authors of the New Testament: **". . . as also our beloved brother Paul, according to the wisdom given him, has written to you..."** (2 Peter 3:15). Peter is upholding Paul.

Between authors of the Old and New Testaments: **"So, all this was done that it might be fulfilled which was spoken by the Lord through the prophet Isaiah saying..."** (Matthew 1:22). Matthew is endorsing Isaiah.

Each was confessing that the "source" of his own information, (the Lord), was also the "source" of the previous authors, even if they wrote many hundreds of years earlier. This "source" then supervised the writing of the whole Bible, and therefore had to live for at least 1,400 years! That is not within the realm of human achievement.

The writing of the Judeo-Christian scripture is also amazing and beyond human capability—"supernatural."

These are all awe-inspiring and have qualities to even dazzle an honest inquirer. This is one reason it is difficult for me to give weight to the pluralist, who wants to treat all these features as if they were mundane enough to be impugned. What are the characteristics and credentials he can produce for himself, that would be impressive enough for me to accept his pronouncements on a par with those having such marks of distinction? Each religion has a brilliance of its own, and each has the right to stake its claim to being the only way. To simply lump them together as a homogenized mixture is not doing justice to the outstanding features they portray. It is the honest response to say, "WOW!" to each feature described in this chapter.

6

Highest Claim

We often think of claims as inferior to fact: a little hollow and lacking in substance. But we rely on them heavily when we are making decisions. I just bought a laptop computer and was looking at the printed slip which described the features. I really had no idea whether the hard drive possessed the capacity, or the system the speed, that the slip claimed. Yet I paid the price and brought it home. We do this numerous times a day in various situations. Bold claims, especially written ones, give us some assurance that what sources are saying is true.

I decided to compare the highest claim that the flesh-and-blood founders made for themselves. I was going to take them at face value without questioning their veracity because, just as in the case of my computer, I had no way of either confirming or refuting them.

A. **Hinduism**: No single founder exists, but Hinduism does have a host of authors. The highest claim of the authors was that of a sage—one respected and revered for his knowledge, integrity, piety, and exceptional insight into spiritual matters.

B. **Islam**: Muhammad was called the "Seal of the Prophets." Islamic tradition tells us that Allah sent down 124,000 prophets, beginning from Adam; but Muhammad was the final one, whose words could not be disputed.

C. **Buddhism**: Gautama Buddha claimed to be the super-enlightened one. After a search for six years, he was enlightened, in stages, during one night, while under a fichus tree in Bodh Gaya, India.

D. **Judaism**: Moses was the acclaimed prophet of Jehovah and the lawgiver in Israel.

E. **Christianity**: Jesus claimed to be the Son of God.

Even a cursory glance revealed that while every claim was great and awesome, the claim of Jesus was "out of this world," literally. All the others were in the human realm; His was in the realm of "God." The others claimed to have some contact with that dimension; Jesus claimed to belong to that dimension. The difference was too stark to miss. When the people of His day heard it, they exclaimed, "Is this not the carpenter's son? Don't we know his siblings?"

The first response was of disbelief. Our first instinct is to dismiss it as a figure of speech or some other non-literal expression. But the more I looked at it in the writings, the clearer it became that that was exactly what He was claiming to be—God! But whoever heard of an ordinary peasant claiming to be God? Would it be worth the time to even try to disprove it?

Yet I realized one thing—this was the highest claim anyone could possibly make. No other founder had made it. If I was looking for some difference between the various claims, then here was a clear-cut one. And however unbelievable it sounded, it was written in the best attested piece of ancient literature. It was truly enigmatic—I realized how unbelievable it would sound to a rational thinker, yet it was not found in a mythological story. I could in no way accept it wholeheartedly—or reject it without proper reason. Claiming to be an inquirer, I had no option but to treat it with respect, not disdain, and check it out calmly.

Frivolity aside, what kind of people would think of making such an outrageous claim?

Four kinds, I'll suggest:

1. Lunatics.
2. Liars/impostors.
3. Megalomaniacs.
4. God.

Did Jesus fit in with any kind?

1. Lunatic. Was He crazy—deluded with visions of grandeur—imagining Himself to be far above what He really was? The word pictures of deluded individuals are usually disjointed thoughts and absurd scenes that keep flitting from one to another, in which they are always riding the crest of the wave. But I had not found a single scholar seriously charging Him with insanity.

On the contrary, many were in awe of His deep and sublime teachings.

> **"Everything in Christ astonishes me . . . the nearer I approach, the more carefully I examine, everything is above me— everything remains grand, of a grandeur which overpowers . . . Neither history, nor humanity, nor the ages, nor nature offer me anything with which I am able to compare or explain it. Here everything is extraordinary"** (Napolean Bonaparte, quoted in McDowell, *New Evidence*, p. 161).

Regarding the words of Jesus:

> **"They are read more, quoted more, loved more, believed more, and translated more because they are the greatest words ever spoken. And where is their greatness? Their greatness lies in the pure lucid spirituality in dealing clearly, definitively and authoritatively with the greatest problems that throb in the human breast."** Bernard

Ramm, *Protestant Christian Evidences* (Chicago, IL: Moody Press, 1953), pp. 170, 171.

No, it would not be fair to label Him "mad."

2. Liar/Impostor. All of His teachings had an undergirding of ethics and morals that won the admiration of some of His harshest critics. To accuse Him of consistently lying at a fundamental point would go against the grain of His entire life and message. Transparent honesty and truthfulness were the major themes of His life.

Yet one must concede that anybody can resort to falsehood at critical moments. None of us has been spared that temptation. But at precisely such a moment, we find a pointer to the extent of His commitment to what He believed. The scene is the trial before the Sanhedrin. One final question would wrap up the proceedings. Placing Jesus under the ultimate oath, to a Jewish ear, the chief priest asks, "Tell us, are you the Son of God?" (The very question I was asking 2,000 years later.) He knew only too well the consequences. To answer in the affirmative would bring upon Himself the instant charge of blasphemy and the punishment of death—exactly what these guardians of the law had been scheming for and desperately working toward for a long time.

People go to great lengths to produce truthful evidence to escape the death sentence. Others have been known to fall back to any form of pretense and falsehood to avoid the death sentence. But no one in his right mind has been known to cling to falsehood and lie under oath to hang himself. Jesus answered in the affirmative and brought upon Himself the death sentence. No higher evidence can exist for the truthfulness of this man. He was not crazy, nor was He a liar. He had to believe, from the depths of His heart, that He was the Son of God.

3. Megalomaniac. The pharaohs of Egypt and the emperors of Rome were examples of those who demanded worship as gods, on pain of severe punishment and even death. These, they did not hesitate to mete out, because they had absolute power, including military power, in their hands. What was this man's position and military power? He had none. Did He constantly make demands for self-aggrandizement? Consider His words, **"I came to serve and not to be served." " . . . to minister and not to be ministered unto."**

In the east, even today, there is a custom of washing the feet of a guest who has come home. Usually, it is the one lowest in the social ladder on whom the task falls. Once, Jesus and His disciples arrived at a home, and there was no servant to wash their feet. Each looked at the other, wondering who would stoop to this lowliest of jobs.

Silently, this man rose up, took off His outer garments, wrapped Himself with a towel, and taking a basin of water, washed the dirty feet of His disciples. No megalomaniac has ever been known to bow before his followers in such humility. Then He turned to His disciples and admonished them to wash one another's feet. Teaching and example dove-tailed into a portrait, not of a bloated ego, but of self-abnegation. This is not the picture of one drunk with power.

4. God. Really and truly God. This is the only option now left. But it is not easy to swallow. Could it be true that this "next-door neighbor" belongs to the realm of God? He appears too ordinary, and belief struggles to accept the claim. But the question persists, however weakly or strongly: "Could it be true?"

Some try a compromise. He was not a deceiver; He was just honestly mistaken. **"A fourth possibility, almost too obvious to need mentioning, is that Jesus was honestly mistaken. Plenty of people are"** (Richard Dawkins, *The God Delusion*, 2006, p. 92). This is a totally unrealistic explanation. One can be honestly mistaken about where the pen was left or regarding a face in a crowd, but not regarding being the Queen of England or having just landed on Mars! Honestly mistaken about being God? That is being ludicrous!

Others want to give the maximum that common sense will allow: He was a good and great man, prophet, and moral teacher, but not God. But His claim was unequivocal—that of being God. As someone said, "If He is not God, He is not good" (St. Anslem).

> **"I am trying here to prevent anyone saying the really foolish thing that people often say about Him: 'I'm ready to accept Jesus as a great moral teacher, but I don't accept His claim to be God.' That is the one thing we must not say. A man who was merely a man and said the sort of things Jesus said would not be a great moral teacher. He would either be a lunatic—on a level with the man who says he is a poached egg—or else he would be the Devil of Hell. You must make your choice. Either this man was, and is, the Son of God: or else a mad man or something worse. You can shut Him up for a fool, you can spit at Him and kill Him as a demon; or you can fall at His feet and call Him Lord and God. But let us not come up with any patronizing nonsense about His being a great human teacher. He has not left that open to us. He did not intend to."** C. S. Lewis, *Mere Christianity* (New York: Macmillan, 1952), pp. 40, 41.

Whether we accept the claim to be true or not, it has to be conceded that Jesus made the highest claim, as compared to any other founder. And because He did not fit easily and smoothly into the categories of ordinary humans known to have claimed a supernatural status, I could not dismiss His claim.

7

Message and Mission

Each founder had a unique story and a specific message to give. Each had a claim as to how the message came and why there was a need for that message. This topic was too cumbersome to explore in much detail. So I decided to put the idea from each founder in a nutshell, in a sentence or two, and then lay them side-by-side for a comparison.

A. **Hinduism:** The sages and authors formed a philosophy to show the way to ultimate truth, which is the merging of the human *atma* (spirit) into the Super Soul or Brahman, to break the cycle of life and death.

B. **Buddhism: "For enlightenment I was born, for the good of all that lives."** Gautama Buddha wanted to pass on the "light," which was ultimate truth, which in turn was ultimate nothingness.

C. **Islam: "For Muslims it (The Quran) is the infallible word of God ... revealed to the Prophet Muhammad by the Angel Gabriel"** (translation of the Quran, by N. J. Dawood, Introduction, p. ix.) The intent was to grasp and spread the word of God to the world.

D. **Judaism: "You shall therefore keep My statutes and My judgments, which if a man does, he shall live..."** (Leviticus 18:5). The key was to establish a set of the correct rules, treat it as a law, and obey it implicitly, to gain life.

E. **Christianity: "I am the way, the truth and the life"** (John 14:6). **"I am the light of the world"** (John 8:12). **"I am the resurrection and the life"** (John 11:25).

The words "I Am" are unique. They are not found in the claims of any other founder. Every other founder could mark out the path, point to the method or way, and insist on showing and expounding the truth which was given to him. This man claimed to *be* the truth. He was not just bringing a message; he *was* the message. Nobody else ever claimed to be identical with the message they were bringing. In all the religions, it was the rules, regulations, and precepts that were taught. Here, it was a *person* who was being introduced—the person who claimed to have established the rules Himself. The difference is like reading a manual to fix a supercomputer, or having the master designer himself ready to consult and guide.

Every other founder claimed to have some contact with the "other world," from whence they got their light, truth, and realizations. Buddha had to search for enlightenment. This was a confession that light was not inherent in him. Muhammad was revealed "the Word" by the angel Gabriel. This was a tacit admission that without this revelation, he would have had nothing to say. Moses clearly stated that all that he ever passed on to the Israelite nation had come from Jehovah. He had nothing of himself to give.

- If you take away the person of Muhammad, Islam and Allah will still remain.
- If you take away the person of Buddha, Buddhism still remains.
- If you take away Moses, Judaism remains.
- If you take away Valmiki and Vyas, Hinduism remains.
- If you take away Jesus, nothing is left of Christianity.

Jesus was making not just a different claim, although the difference is stark, but was also speaking from a position which He claimed to be significantly and radically different.

Let me illustrate it with two comparisons.

First, consider Gautama Buddha. Until the age of 29, he was not enlightened at all. He spent the next six years in a relentless, desperate search. He tried various methods and ways.

> **"To such a pitch of asceticism have I gone that naked was I, flouting life's decencies . . . I have visited only one house a day and there taken only one morsel . . . or one every seven days, or only once a fortnight . . . I have plucked out the hair of my head and the hair of my beard. . . having couched on thorns . . . in diverse fashions, I have lived to torment and to torture my body, to such a length of asceticism have I gone"** (Chen, *Buddhism the Light of Asia*, 1968, p. 21).

Finally, after this rigorous penance, he attained enlightenment one night, going through four successive stages of realizations. Even after that, he was not sure what to do with that "light" and had to be coaxed by "Brahma" to go ahead and deliver the message. In short, it was an all-consuming struggle to reach a goal. Let us grant that he did reach it. Compare this search and uncertainty with the story of Jesus.

Jesus did not need to struggle. We have no record of any desperate, torturous search for truth and light. He was never in a quandary regarding His claims. He simply said, "I *am* the light." He did not strain every nerve to reach the goal of truth—he *was* the goal. And from that vantage position, He claimed to describe truth.

Second, let's focus on Muhammad. One of the most spiritual experiences described in his life was the "Night Journey." This is cited as a powerful claim to his status as the "Seal of the Prophets." In the year 620, he was taken one night from Mecca on the heavenly steed Buruq to the Temple mount in Jerusalem.

There, a ladder was set up, on which he and Gabriel climbed through the seven heavens to the level of the throne of Allah. He returned to earth the same night. He was thus given an exalted privilege of having been in proximity to the essence of Allah. Although there is some controversy whether this was a physical or mystical journey, let us grant that he did have this incredible experience.

Inherent in this description is the confession that Muhammad belonged to this earth, and he was allowed to travel up to heaven as a visitor for a brief glance. Contrast this with the claims of Jesus. Heaven, that wondrous place, was His dwelling place. He belonged there and had to come down to earth as a visitor for a specific purpose. *The origins and directions of travel between the two stand in exact reverse.*

Who would know more about New York City and the finer details about its hectic life among the jostling crowds of Manhattan—one who has lived there all his life, or one who flew in from India and took a guided tour of the city for a few hours before hopping onto the next flight heading home? If truth resided in your home, you would know it the best!

If we accept the claim that Buddha was enlightened and that Muhammad had the Night Journey, it would only be fair to accept the claim that Jesus came down from heaven, bringing the message in Himself, and that He occupied the unique position from which He alone could state the truth from a supernatural dimension and angle. He therefore had every right to say, "I Am." The claim clearly sets Him apart from the others.

8

Teaching Versus Life

By precept and example."

"By word and deed."

"Actions speak louder than words."

"What you are doing is so loud that I cannot hear what you are saying."

Consistency in the life of an individual—that's what makes a greater impact than any profession of the lips. The teachings the founders brought were all wonderful and deep, but what I wanted to know was whether their own life-actions had been brought into line with those teachings. This, to me, was the *acid test* of the profession of the founders. They claimed to be the leaders. Did they lead by word only or by action as well, and to what extent?

This was one area in which, because of the nature of the question, I had to be somewhat negative and look for faults and inconsistencies. I tried to balance that by comparing the record of their lives with their own teachings. That way, *their own teachings* were the pointing finger, and I did not have to define what was right or wrong for them. Their writings did that and effectively kept my private evaluations at bay.

A. **Hinduism: "When a man gives up all varieties of desire for sense gratification, . . . then he is said to be in pure transcendental consciousness"** (Bhagavad-Gita, 2:55).

"A person who is not disturbed by the incessant flow of desires . . . can alone achieve peace" (Bhagavad-Gita, 2:70).

The desires mentioned here are varied but definitely include sensual, sexual desires.

"Our holy books tell us of gods, sages and heroes who, though high-minded, were addicted to sensuous passions." These were the words of Gautama Buddha, when, as a Hindu, he reviewed the heroes of the Hindu tradition.

This is well substantiated in the life of Krishna. His sexual exploits with the "gopi's" (milk-maids) of Vrindavana, of whom Radha was his favorite, is common traditional knowledge. He was even chided by Sisupala for this at a royal meeting—**"this is not like stealing the clothes of helpless women when they are bathing in the river. This is not like stealing the loves of Gopi women and cheating their husbands"** (*Mahabharata*, translated by Kamala Subramaniam, Bharataya Vidya Bhavan, 13th Edition, 2004, pp. 169, 170).

Some sources go so far as to say, **"In the course of his life he was supposed to have had 16,108 wives and 180,008 sons."** Benjamin Walker, *Hindu World* (London: George Allen & Unwin, 1968), p. 73.

B. **Buddhism: "Here venerable gentlemen are the four rules about the offenses which deserve expulsion . . . 1) If a monk should have sexual intercourse with anyone."** Edward Conze, *Buddhist Scriptures* (Baltimore: Penguin Books, 1959), p. 73.

When Buddha was born, his father, Sudhodana, the king of the Gotama Clan, was told by a seer that if he wanted his son to be a great world emperor, he would have to keep him from setting his eyes on poverty, old age, disease, or death. In an attempt to fulfill his wish, multi-storied palaces were built, in which Buddha, then known as Siddhartha, was kept on the upper floors so that he would never come down to the palace grounds and thus come into contact with what was prohibited. To keep his mind occupied, he was kept busy by women minstrels:

> **"They entertained him with wanton swayings . . . butterfly kisses and seductive glances. Thus he became a captive of these women who were well-versed in the subject of sensuous enjoyment and indefatigable in sexual pleasure."**
>
> **"On the night of his renunciation he awoke to find the female musicians sleeping . . . some with their bodies wet with trickling phlegm, some with their dress fallen apart so as to plainly disclose their loathsome nakedness."** (Conze, *Buddhist Scriptures*, p. 38.)

This is a description of a sexual orgy. And this had been going on for day after day, month after month, and year after year, for at least thirteen years.

During the years of his search for light, he said, **"I . . . have gone down to the water punctually thrice before nightfall to wash away *the evil within*"** (Chen, *Buddhism, The Light of Asia*, p. 21, italics supplied).

His life was flawed according to his own teachings; what he himself called "evil" was "within" him and needed to be washed away.

C. **Islam: "Then you may marry other women who seem good to you: two, three, or four of them."** (The Quran, 4: 2-4). This is the only place where the number of wives allowed is spelled out in the Quran. The traditional writings say Muhammad had *eleven* wives.

"We have given you a glorious victory so that God may forgive your past and future *sins*" (The Quran, 48:1, italics supplied).

"Did He not find you in *error* and guide you?" (The Quran, 93:6, italics supplied).

Muhammad is acknowledged as the "perfect man" by Muslim tradition.

Obviously, this refers to the highest level that a human can possibly attain, "sins" and "error" notwithstanding; for whatever the writings considered "sins" were found in him. And whatever the degree of guilt, he needed forgiveness for them.

The ideal, as depicted in the writings, was still beyond him.

D. **Judaism: "Thou shalt not kill. . . . Thou shalt not commit adultery . . . . Thou shalt not bear false witness."** Moses was guilty of murder. **"So he looked this way and that and when he saw no one, he killed him"** (Exodus 2:12). Later on in the wilderness, he expressly disobeyed God, who had told him to speak to, not strike, the rock. This offense was sufficient to keep him from going into the Promised Land, one of his most cherished dreams.

Abraham committed adultery. **"So he went in to Hagar and she conceived"** (Genesis 16:4). Hagar was not his wife, Sarah was. This towering patriarch also stumbled at the point of falsehood, when he told a "white lie" to escape the Egyptians.

David committed adultery. **"Then David sent messengers and took her"** (2 Samuel 11:4). This refers to Bathsheba, who was not his wife. And worse, he had the husband killed, in what can only be described as premeditated, cold-blooded murder (2 Samuel 11:15).

None of these three Hebrew "greats" was able to keep his record clean.

E. **Christianity: Here are twelve testimonials regarding Jesus.**

1. Pilate was a Roman governor. No love was lost between the Romans and the Jews, and Jesus was a Jew. Yet this is what Pilate said: **"And indeed having examined in your presence, I have found no fault in this man."** (Luke 23:14). **"I find no fault in him *at all*"** (John 18:38, italics supplied).

2. Herod was a king in the region. Pilate referred to him as also not having found any fault in Christ. **"Neither did Herod, for I sent you back to him"** (Luke 23:15).

3. Pilate's wife sent him a note during the trial of Jesus, cautioning him about the defendant and describing Him as **"that *just* man"** (Matthew 27:19).

4. A Roman centurion at the cross exclaimed, **"Certainly this was a *righteous* man"** (Luke 23:47, italics supplied).

5. One of the felons crucified alongside Jesus turned to another, who

was also crucified, and—acknowledging their own guilt, for which they were being punished—confessed whatever he knew about Jesus, saying, "**. . . but this man has done nothing wrong**" (Luke 23:41).

These had probably seen Him from a distance or had only heard of Him. How about those who knew Him intimately?

6. John was the closest to Jesus among the disciples. He had probably watched Him closely from morning to evening, day after day, for over three years, and then he decided that **"in him is no sin"** (1 John 3:5).
7. Peter was another of the three closest disciples. He, too, reached the same conclusion and portrayed Christ as **"without blemish and without spot"** (1 Peter 1:19).
8. Probably it was Paul who compared Him to us, saying that Jesus "**. . . was in all points tempted as we are, yet without sin**" (Hebrews 4:15).
9. This next disciple, Judas, was apparently disloyal, but after betraying Christ, confessed, **"I have sinned by betraying innocent blood"** (Matthew 27:4).
10. Jesus is the only founder of a world religion who has been acknowledged in the writings of another world religion. He is mentioned in ninety-three verses in the Quran: Multiple times He is identified as the son of Mary, and nearly a dozen times He is called the Messiah. Surah 3, verse 46 (speaking of Jesus), says, **"He shall preach to men . . . in the prime of manhood and shall lead a *righteous* life."** A significant testimony!
11. The words of Jesus Himself were nothing short of startling. Facing bitter opponents who were thirsting for His death, He asked, "Which of you convicts me of sin?" The answer was silence. To look within and find nothing wrong is completely foreign to the human experience. Nobody I know has been able to look into his life record to find an absolutely clean slate. The best of us have such a dismal record that sometimes the very thought of it chokes us with shame and humiliation. Even the highly revered K'ung Ch'iu (more commonly known as Confucius, the founder of Confucianism) confessed, **"How dare I claim to be a sage or a benevolent man."** Confucius, *The Analects* (Penguin Books, 1979),

back cover. In this context, the self-conscious purity of Jesus should be taken as a surpassing marvel.

12. Finally, consider the trial of Jesus. In the Hebrew tradition, the Sanhedrin was not only the highest religious authority but also the judicial body making decisions in civil and criminal cases. In small matters, a minimum of three members could make up the quorum to pass judgment. In crucial, major issues, the number was to be twenty-three. When it came to matters of national importance, the "full council" of seventy plus the chief priest was required (*Every Man's Talmud*, Abraham Cohen, 1949, pp. 300-302). An indication has it that the "full council" had met for the trial of Jesus, but this cannot be clearly verified. However, the descriptions in the story depict a fairly large number.

The principle behind the different levels of quorum was to ensure the maximum talent and information and the less likelihood of judicial blunders in matters of greater importance.

The trial began with bringing in witnesses to see if Jesus could be condemned. As the trial went on, it became clearer and clearer that the evidence was not forthcoming—the charges of breaking the law could not be substantiated. Then the high priest himself (going against the law—he was not supposed to play any part in accusing the defendant) examined Jesus. Placing Him under the most solemn oath to the Jewish ear, he and the council demanded the answer to the question of whether He really claimed to be the Son of God. **"Are you then the Son of God?"** (Luke 22:70.) The answer sent Jesus to His death. The judicial process had yielded a clear sentence of conviction, but the significant point was the shift from deed to identity. The question had moved from what He had or had not done to who He claimed to be. Why the change? Because the whole council, bringing *all the evidence* they were capable of producing, could find nothing wrong in what He had ever done. In these judicial proceedings lies one of the highest forms of evidence of the innocence of this man.

Taking the whole spectrum of testimonials, it is difficult to claim bias, friendship, kinship, or any other factor as the basis of the confessions, other than the truth about that stainless life. And just as in the trial, held so long ago and which yielded a clear conviction, so my question now regarding the life record of the founders had yielded an undeniable result.

Here alone did I find a life in which the theory had been matched in practice, where the teachings had found their complete fulfillment in a real-life performance. I had to salute this feat of an unblemished thirty-three years that had met the strictest scrutiny from those who pursued Him to His death. I had to confess that here alone stood an individual who could look everyone in the eye and, with perfect right and credibility, say, "Follow me." No other founder could legitimately make such a claim.

A Pause

At this point, I stopped to assess the picture, and it looked too one-sided. This book and this man, Jesus, appeared favored and too dominant. Was I pushing His story up unfairly and forcing Him out to the forefront of the race? Was I choosing only the topics that put Him at the top? If I was doing that, I would ultimately be the one who would stand to lose. I did become a bit uncomfortable. So I intentionally searched for topics where He would not come out ahead. The next three, (birth, length of ministry, and death) are such. He lands up anywhere but at the head.

9

Birth

Each founder came into this world in an unusual manner. Stories abound regarding those tidbits that are supposed to point to their status as special individuals.

The Hindu authors did not have many intriguing stories around their births, although such descriptions were numerous in the older unverifiable writings regarding the deities.

Buddha was born after his mother, Maya, had a white elephant miraculously enter her body from one side. When it came time for giving birth, the baby came out in a painless manner from the side of her body and not from the birth passage. The first thing the baby did was declare his mission of enlightenment and then take seven steps, with a lotus flower growing out of the ground at every step.

Muhammad was born with a special mark between his shoulder blades that identified his exalted status. When he was turned over to another family who had the task of nursing him, the milk began to flow miraculously and in copious amounts not only from the "wet nurse" but also from their camel, which had been "dry" before but was finally able to provide enough nourishment and sustenance for that family.

Moses was born to slaves, who placed him in a basket and let it float among the bulrushes in a strategic part of the River Nile, where the Pharaoh's daughter came to bathe. She picked him up, took him to the palace, and adopted him into her own family. *Moses* means "drawn out of water."

Jesus was born to Mary, who claimed to be a virgin despite the pregnancy. The special birth was first announced to some lowly shepherds out on the hillsides who were watching over their sheep at night. A glorious angel suddenly appeared and told of the birth and was immediately joined by a choir of shining beings who sang of God's gift to the human race.

Fascinating accounts, all of them. But I was looking for the points at which Jesus would not be placed higher than the others.

A. **Hinduism:** No single person is the founder; instead, multiple authors created their writings. All of them appear to have been revered individuals born to parents with prestige and honor surrounding them.

B. **Buddhism:** Gautama Buddha, known as Siddhartha, was a prince. His father, Suddhodana, and his mother, Maya, were king and queen of the Gotama clan in northern India. He was born in Lumbini Grove amid great celebrations welcoming the new heir to the throne (Conze, *Buddhist Scriptures*, p. 35). His was a stately beginning.

C. **Judaism: "A man of the house of Levi went and took as wife, a daughter of Levi ... bore a son and she saw that he was a beautiful child ... and he became her [Pharaoh's daughter's] son"** (Exodus 2:1, 10). The tribe of Levi was prestigious, because it was later to be in charge of the tabernacle, the most sacred possession of the nation. His reputable pedigree was not only in the native sense but also by adoption.

D. **Islam:** Muhammad was the **"posthumous son of Abdullah... his mother Amina ... of the tribe of Quraysh, clan of Hashim"** (Armstrong, *Muhammad*, p. 19). The tribe of Quraysh was not the strongest or largest tribe among the Arabians, but it was very important, because it was the guardian of the Kaba, the most sacred site on the peninsula. This connection was a matter of pride and distinction to the family and also to Muhammad.

E. **Christianity: "After his mother Mary was betrothed to Joseph, before they came together she was found with child"** (Matthew 1:18); **". . . and wrapped him in swaddling clothes, and laid him in a manger, because there was no room in the inn"** (Luke 2:7).

Two features become evident:

- Jesus was the only founder to be born in poverty-stricken circumstances—among the lowly beasts of the field; wrapped in cheap, coarse cloth; and laid in a feeding trough amid the stench and squalor of a cattle shed.

- And worse, He was the only founder to be born an illegitimate child.

Look over the descriptions of the birth stories again. Jesus was the only founder conceived out of wedlock! In today's world, this might not amount to much, but in first-century Palestine, in that ultra-conservative society, this was not an acceptable status. The individual was morally stained, as well as the whole family, and this fact was considered an indication that the favor of God was not on them. It was a ready cause for taunts and jeers. Nor was it something that Jesus could hide or deny. It dogged His days from His youth and on through the years of His ministry. In fact, when He went to the temple, the religious top brass and educated elite dismissed Him with disdain: "We were not born of fornication!"

In other words, "Who are you? And despite how you were born, you pretend to teach the people? And morals and ethics—of all things! You—you are a bastard. (The word is used in the traditional writings of the Jews. See McDowell, *The New Evidence That Demands a Verdict*, p. 304.) "We," they said, "are not! You have no business here among the clean and the favored of God. Just get out of here!"

How's that for a start in attempting to build a religious tradition! Of all the founders, Christ's was certainly the worst entry and the worst beginning for a religious cause. On this point, Jesus comes out last—last by a long mile.

Yet, some questions remain. How was it that He managed to develop a following, despite such a deep, permanent moral stain on His name? Did something else over-ride this factor?

Another question loomed up, on reflection: He claimed to be the Son of God. The people, on the other hand, described Him as illegitimate, because nobody could identify His father, either in the village or elsewhere. What if the reason was because His father was really God? So that awful label, meant to hound and humiliate, could have been an unwitting admission that His claim might be a possibility. What if His Father really was God? What if . . . ?

10

Length of Ministry

The tenure of a leader usually has some reflection on his staying power. This, in turn, could relate to the way that society, in general, accepts the person or his teachings. It could also reflect shrewdness, personality, and political power or position—along with any endearing quality that he possessed. We naturally tend to respect those who have been at the helm a long time. Admiration rises as the period lengthens.

How did the founders fare on this point?

A. **Hinduism:** The authors of the various writings lived over a great period of time. Hindu thought developed over many generations. During that time, an organized society was formed, with different levels of value for individuals, their birth and parentage, their occupations, etc. It turned out to be a vast, complicated system of philosophy and religious practice. This process continued for centuries, and then, millennia. Today, there are close to a billion professors of the Hindu faith.

B. **Islam:** Prophet Muhammad received his first vision in the year 610 C.E. (Common Era— the same as A.D.). His last message was given to him in the year of his demise in 632 C.E. During those twenty-three years, he gradually, and with tremendous courage and determination, built up a following and an army that not only protected the Muslims but allowed for military conquests, which finally resulted in the formation of the mighty Ottoman Empire. A combination of religious, political, and military power built the giant edifice for the Muslims. The base was the decades of Muhammad's own contribution, in terms of religious and military leadership. Today, there is a vast population of over one billion Muslims, and that number is growing rapidly.

C. **Buddhism:** At the age of 35, after six years of intensive search for light, Gautama Buddha began to preach the initial principles of Buddhism. The first sermon was at Varanasi, in northern India. His last sermon was given at the age of 80 in Kusinara. Those forty-five years were spent in an extremely active and tireless effort of teaching, preaching, and traveling extensively.

The later years included organizing the followers into groups called *sanghas,* which formed the foundation of the monasteries that were established to practice and spread the faith. Today, there is a string of monasteries over the land-mass of southeast Asia and a growing population of 405 million Buddhists.

D. **Judaism:** Moses began to lead the children of Israel at the age of 80 and held control till he died at 120. The whole venture was a severe trial for him, because the initial group, numbering in the hundreds of thousands, was made up of slaves who had been such for generations. They had no place to call home, so they were constantly on the move for forty years, hoping to get to the place they called the "Promised Land." Painstakingly, he molded them, using the principles given him on Mt. Sinai, into an organized nation with specific religious rites, a civil and health code, and a well-trained army. It took the full forty years to transform that rag-tag but idealistic group into a nation governed by precise rules and laws.

E. **Christianity:** The number drastically falls. Jesus traversed the regions of Galilee spreading His message and miracles for a mere three and a half years. This striking difference naturally elicits the question, "Why?" And the answer reveals a truly pathetic picture. His years were cut short by a rejection from His community that was so severe and total that it ended in death.

Let us look at those numbers again. It's not a wide spectrum, with Jesus inside the middle of the continuum. No, He's at the tail-end. All the founders had decades to develop their thought—enough time, spanning a generation or more, to improve, refine, and then expound on the message. All of them could look back with a sense of satisfaction on an illustrious career, the influence of which was changing the very landscape. They had made a statement to the world, and it was gaining acceptance everywhere and clearly taking root in society. Hurrah!

Not so with Jesus. This man had only three and a half years. His time was that short because He was hated with a passion by many in His community and country, booted out with contempt, and finally condemned to die as a criminal. Unquestionably, Jesus comes out last on this point, too. Who would be impressed with such a résumé!

Yet some questions remain. How long does it take to make a statement to the world—twenty-three to forty-five, versus three and a half years? Jesus was only a carpenter-turned-itinerant preacher, from a tiny, unknown village in a country that had no political standing, except as annexed to another kingdom. His main audience was usually a motley group of fishermen, common folk, and curious onlookers. Why should He be remembered at all, let alone revered and worshiped? Why hasn't time wiped off those short years from history?

Others with greater exploits and accomplishments have long since vanished from the horizon. Why does Jesus, having had the shortest period and the most obscure livelihood, yet now, 2,000 years later, have the greatest following the world has ever known?

11

Death

The ending, the *coup de grace,* of any event or life is nearly always looked upon as a defining moment. A certain power arrests attention when watching that finale. From the short, hundred-meter dash to the long-drawn-out and grueling marathon, everything along the way recedes into the background when compared to what happens at the tape. The triumph and the pathos, the ecstasy and the disappointment, the making and the breaking—all are focused there. That is where everything seemed to be headed, but we had to wait for that climactic point to see what it really was all about. Always bewitching—and always gripping.

A. **Hinduism:** The Hindu masters and sages were revered and held in high esteem. At the culmination of their lives, they and their families were widely praised and honored for the blessing they had brought to the community.

   Their deaths were regarded as significant losses, to be lamented over for generations, as their lives were recounted over and over again. The masters themselves passed on the baton (of religious thought) with flair, as each expanded upon the labors of their predecessors.

B. **Buddhism:** Gautama died surrounded by his doting disciples, who strained to catch every one of his last words. They described the moment vividly: "When the sage entered nirvana, the earth quivered like a ship struck by a squall and fire-brands fell from the sky . . . the body was wrapped in one thousand layers of finest Benares cloth and cremated." The cloth was the famed silk from Benares (Varanasi) and was meant to portray the highest honor possible. His task was done; he had rounded up his teachings on enlightenment. And now it was left to the followers to continue the good work.

C. **Islam:** When Umar, one of the prominent leaders, heard of Muhammad's demise, he said, "I was dumb-founded... I fell to the ground." The people hurried, ashen-faced, to the mosque. The time-honored practice of women beating their breasts was seen throughout the town. Their greatest leader had gone, and even though grief-stricken, they were going to express their profound respect and admiration.

   Everywhere were heard words describing that grand and extraordinary life. Muhammad had built the framework for the juggernaut of the caliphate that would later sweep the world and bring almost every opposition to its knees.

D. **Judaism: "Moses was one hundred and twenty years old when he died . . . and the children of Israel wept for Moses in the plains of Moab for thirty days"** (Deuteronomy 34:7, 8). The entire nation came to a halt and stayed paralyzed for thirty days. This was a show of great respect, much as when we declare a period of state mourning and fly the national flag at half-mast, when a president has died in office. Moses had taken the wandering nation of Israel—the males alone numbering over 600,000—to the brink of the Promised Land, the land "flowing with milk and honey." That feat of leadership and organizational skills has remained a marvel to this day.

E. **Christianity: "With him were also crucified two robbers, one on his right and the other on his left . . . and he was numbered with the transgressors . . . At the ninth hour Jesus cried out with a loud voice saying, ' My God, my God, why have you forsaken me'"** (Mark 15: 27-34).

Christ ended His life stripped stark naked, pinned to an instrument of torture (like the roaches I used to dissect in school), with lacerated skin, bleeding head and limbs, and a spear thrust into His torso. Rejected and reviled, harassed and humiliated, He bore a gut-wrenching sorrow that finally broke His heart.

What a difference! What an incredible contrast! He was not just last in the line, He was in a different line altogether; in a different category—by far the worst!

But the greater the difference, the more the questions that tended to rise:

1. Why was it that when He led, it was by a big margin, and then when He lagged behind, He was so far away as to be out of sight?
2. Why would composers of some of the greatest symphonies choose topics from His life as a theme? Were the topics from this *criminal* so captivating?
3. What made some of the finest artists and sculptors contemplate and then complete their works, with His message as their inspiration?
4. Was there an explanation for the fact that some of the great institutions of learning, in scores of countries all over the world, started out in His name? Who would want the name of a common criminal to adorn the central structures of their institutions?
5. The largest task force undertaking humanitarian projects world-wide

is the body of people who call themselves by His name. Taken together throughout history, in all wars and natural disasters, no other group has been able to match the rapidity, the effectiveness, the zeal and self sacrifice, of those who go by that name. What drives them—a condemned criminal dying a horrible death? That wouldn't make much sense, would it?

6. Look at the lengths to which the followers are willing to go. I have seen them with my own eyes—living in huts and hovels, eating the food of those they serve, drinking their water, contracting their diseases, facing the loss of loved ones and babies, and finally, dying just like any of the others in those dirty, poverty-stricken villages—unknown and unrecognized and lying today under little mounds of dirt without even a nametag nearby. What, in the name of anything, causes them to do this? Why point to a naked, tortured body on a cross? Why not to an emperor or military general or some wealthy business tycoon who could guarantee security to the family once they were gone?

7. What if, at the peak of his life, Muhammad was found guilty and condemned to death? What if Gautama Buddha, near the summit of his life, was convicted and sentenced to hang?

   I think such culminations in the stories of their lives would have also been the end of all their moral and ethical undertakings. The rank and file would have quickly abandoned them in disappointment and disgust, and we would not have had Islam or Buddhism today. Jesus was condemned and hanged; His followers left Him and fled. Why should there be Christianity today?

8. The Jewish priests specifically demanded death by crucifixion. There appeared to be a calculated plan behind it. In the books of law, the Torah, in Deuteronomy 21:23, it is written that if the punishment of death was to be by hanging, it would signify that the person had been cursed by God. That body was to be buried before sundown, because if left above ground, it would pollute the land—so vile and contemptible was the person. This amounted to incontrovertible evidence of His terrible guilt, affirmed by God Himself. His bitter cry on the cross, of being abandoned, only further testified to that God-forsaken state. So he died a criminal, condemned by the highest religious authority in the nation, the Sanhedrin; by the highest civil and judicial authority in the world, the Romans; and by the highest authority in the universe to the Jewish mind—God.

No noble, lasting cause had ever been birthed at such an ignoble ending of a founder. Yet the first converts to Christianity were Jews, and some of them were priests. What made those first Jewish priests, well-versed in the Torah, choose to follow Him, despite such a dismal record? What could have been weightier and more powerful than the pronouncements by the highest religious and civil authorities of His day?

9. No other story has inspired the writing of so much religious literature as the record of this man's life, as found in the Gospels. Christian books, periodicals, encyclopedias, poems, verses, songs, and research papers, form the greatest bulk of literary works in the world today, and they are all essentially inspirational, ethical, and moral in nature.

   If He ended up as a blasphemer and was ultimately forsaken of God, why should anyone listen to and embrace *His* ideas of ethics and morals? The record would have shown how morally bankrupt He really was. This disclosure would have silenced everyone, including those cowardly disciples of His who ran at the first hint of trouble when He was about to be arrested, then later changed their minds and spoke and wrote so boldly about Him. Why did they change their minds?

10. If Jesus was just a felon who had finally met a deservedly damned ending to an insignificant but blasphemous life, why has history been split in two by Him—B.C. (Before Christ) and A.D. (*Anno Domini,* meaning "the year of our Lord")? What reason to put Him in that pivotal position and leave Him there for 2,000 years? Was nobody else on the horizons of human history found to have better credentials than this crucified criminal?

"But to believe that a remote impostor, in a forgotten province of a perished empire, stamped Himself so deeply on Time as to compel all the centuries to bear His name is to believe that a child, with its box of colors could change the tint of all the oceans!" W. H. Fitchett, *The Unrealized Logic of Religion* (London: Charles H. Kelley, 1905), p. 26.

There has to be more to the story. We must press on to find it.

12

POST-DEATH

What happened after the founder had died? How was the momentum of the movement sustained? In most cases, there was a tearful farewell, followed by the construction of a shrine to keep the memory of the beloved leader alive. The void within the group caused by the death was then filled by choosing another leader so that the movement did not suffer or disappear.

A. **Hinduism:** Many leaders and authors were spread over generations. What usually followed death was cremation, with great mourning, on the one hand—or celebrations with feasting, on the other. The remains from the cremation—the ashes—were scattered over and into the River Ganges, the holiest of rivers, signifying a merger with the eternal. Memorials and shrines then came up in their honor.

B. **Buddhism: "For some days they worshiped the relics . . . with utmost devotion . . . divided them into eight parts. One they kept for themselves. The seven others were handed over to the seven kings . . . they erected in their capital cities stupas (or memorial mounds) for the relics"** (Conze, *Buddhist Scriptures*, p. 65).

C. **Islam:** "Abu Bakr died after only two years and was **succeeded by Umar, then by Uthman. Finally in 656 Ali became the fourth Caliph"** (Armstrong, *Muhammad*, p. 258).

D. **Judaism: "So Moses the servant of the Lord died there in the land of Moab . . ."** (Deuteronomy 34:6).

"After the death of Moses . . . it came to pass that the Lord spoke to Joshua the son of Nun" (Joshua 1:1).

E. **Christianity: "I am He who lives and was dead, and behold I am alive forevermore Amen. And have the keys of Hades and of death"** (Revelation 1:18).

"And lo I am with you always, even to the end of the age" (Matthew 28:20).

Weighing these claims honestly, we must confess that the last one, the Christian claim, is nothing less than stunning. Here is an irreconcilable parting of the ways between the claims of Jesus and those of any other founder. He claims to be alive after being tortured to death.

Why would anyone make such a far-fetched claim? How would He expect anyone to believe such a report—truly and bodily alive, after days of being dead? And to add to that, He is said to have predicted it! The first inclination is to dismiss it as a frivolous concoction (a "pernicious superstition," according to the Roman historian Cornelius Tacitus) or to relegate it to the level of a chimerical myth. Of all the claims in the universe, this must surely be the hardest to seriously entertain. But we must, at this point, discipline ourselves to remain an inquirer, even if it means going against every grain of rational thought. Yes, it is unbelievable, but it is written in the best-attested historical piece of ancient literature in the world and should not be cast away as a myth. That would not be fair. And further, why do so many intelligent, rational, balanced people believe it? What causes them to become so gullible at this one point, or do they really have something to go by? But whoever heard of anyone actually being resurrected from the dead?

Once again, we find ourselves on the horns of a seemingly unsolvable dilemma: unable to believe it, yet unable to confidently reject it.

Our only hope lies in examining the report the best we can. And here we should, first of all, differentiate between an event and the meaning ascribed to it. The meaning that the followers give is clearly a Christian, religious, doctrinal, and philosophical point.

But the event itself is not religious, doctrinal, or philosophical at all but rather, a purely neutral, historical claim.

> **"Whether the resurrection of Jesus took place or not is a historical question—and so the question has to be decided on the level of historical argument"** (Wolfhart Pannenberg, Professor, University of Munich, in *Christianity Today*, April 1968, p. 12).

The question assumes huge dimensions, and we cannot afford to be lackadaisical and sloppy, for **"It is either the greatest miracle or the greatest delusion which history records."** Philip Schaff, *History of the Christian Church*, reprinted (Grand Rapids, MI: William B. Eerdmans, 1962), p. 173.

We will gain nothing by a half-hearted attempt or one that is predetermined. Here, more than at any other part of our search, we must cling to a seeking, learning attitude. To help us remain inquirers, we accept Aristotle's pertinent dictum:

> **"The benefit of the doubt is to be given to the document itself, not arrogated by the critic to himself"** (quoted from McDowell, *New Evidence That Demands a Verdict*, p. 409).

> **"One must listen to the claims of the document under analysis, and not assume fraud or error unless the author disqualifies himself by contradictions or known factual inaccuracies"** (John Montgomery, in *Christianity Today*, August 16, 1968).

The event happened 2,000 years ago. How much information would there be for us today, to sift and weigh out in a reasonable manner?

> **"Let it be simply said that we know more about the details of the hours immediately before and the actual death of Jesus—than we know about the death of any other one man in all the ancient world—We know more about the burial of the Lord Jesus than we know of the burial of any single character in all of ancient history."** Wilbur Smith, *Therefore Stand* (Grand Rapids, MI: Baker Book House, 1945), p. 360.

From a time and age when written descriptions were extremely sparse, and even single sentences regarding kings and emperors have hardly managed to survive, to find this degree of information regarding an ordinary peasant done to death as a disgraced criminal, is truly astonishing. By today's standards, it might be equal to chapters and chapters of a detailed account. So we just might have enough in our hands to make an exploration.

Two essential questions require addressing in an investigation such as ours:

1. If the story is unbelievable, what could the correct story be?
2. If the story is true, are there evidences for it?

The Corrected Report

Why attempt to correct the story? Because it is very difficult to believe. It strains our sense of reasoning. We are unable to give a rational explanation for anyone rising up from the dead. I think we should freely acknowledge this. That being the case, any proposed change should fit in smoothly with the rest of the story. It should not leave obvious gaps, unexplained portions, and big questions, to the point of straining our sense of reasoning again; otherwise, all we would have done is jumped from the frying pan into the fire.

A few alternatives have been proposed, but they can be condensed into two basic theories:

1. He did not die—He only fainted (swoon theory)
2. He died but did not rise—the body was stolen (theft theory)

Swoon Theory

The proposal is that Jesus only fainted on the cross and later recuperated because of the cool, reviving atmosphere in the tomb. Does the written story easily allow this suggestion?

1. **Pilate's cautious approval: "Pilate marveled that he was already dead; and summoning the centurion, he asked him if he had been dead for some time. So when he found out from the centurion, he granted the body to Joseph."** (Mark 15:44, 45). The writer of this Gospel did not know that we were going to ask this question 2,000 years later, yet he has given us bits that directly address our concerns:

    - Pilate marveled. Of course, he would.

      The average time from crucifixion to death is days, not hours. Some struggled on for three to seven days before the prolonged ordeal was over. Jesus died in six hours. Pilate therefore wanted to make sure that death had indeed occurred. It would have been a great mockery if the mighty Roman Empire was shown unable to put to death an ordinary Jewish peasant.

    - He granted the body only after confirming death.

    - He was not satisfied with just a quick glance. He specifically asked if He had been dead *"for some time."*

2. **The spear: "When they came to Jesus and saw that he was already dead, they did not break his legs. But one of the soldiers pierced his side with a spear"** (John 19:33, 34). This was how the centurion made sure He was dead. Realizing that the body made no movement, yet it was too early for death, he was hesitant to bring the body down to be handed over. So he commanded that the issue be firmly settled—with one thrust of a well-trained Roman soldier's spear. If Jesus had not died of crucifixion, He would have certainly died of that thrust. That was what it was meant to accomplish.

3. **Blood and Water: ". . . the soldier pierced his side with a spear, and immediately blood and water came out. And he who has seen has testified"** (John 19:35). The description of two streams is what got my attention. As a physician, I began to look for possible physiological answers. There could be two explanations. One, the blood was mixed with another fluid, such as pericardial fluid (produced by the outer lining of the heart), with the blood itself partially clotting, so as to remain distinct. Second, the cellular elements of blood, such as the red blood corpuscles, settled out to form the red portion, leaving the clear part, the serum, separate. Both these processes require time. Both require

that the blood be still and not moving in circulation. The cells do not settle unless the blood is absolutely motionless. This is one basis of a test that some doctors order, called the ESR (Erythrocyte Sedimentation Rate), for which the patient's blood is drawn into a fine tube and kept absolutely still. The doctors usually order a one-hour or a two-hour ESR, because it takes time for the cells to settle down to leave the upper portion clear.

The spear could have hit at the junction of the two portions, thus causing two streams to flow out. The two streams, therefore, could be taken as a fairly strong indication that the blood had stopped flowing *"for some time,"* the very confirmation of death that Pilate had wanted before giving his assent regarding the body! The fact that John was no modern-day physician and so described it in the terms of an ordinary layman (water instead of serum) gives great credibility to that simple, specific, yet significant observation.

4. **Multiple testimonials:** Christ's own friends, the ones who took Him down from the cross, believed Him to be dead. That is why they arranged for the burial. If they had thought that any hope of life remained, they would not have wanted to embalm the body, which would have required the use of substances that would have made a return to life impossible. So if Pilate, the Roman centurion, as well as the friends of Jesus made irrevocable decisions regarding the state of the body, there is no good reason to question it.

5. **Escape from the tomb:** Is that a reasonable possibility? Christ's wrist bones were probably fractured, so He could not have used His hands. His ankle bones were also fractured, so He could not have walked, let alone run. His body had been thrust through with a Roman spear, not a fine sword or javelin. His back was one huge seeping mass of lacerated skin and flesh. If He still had been alive, this would have been the time for the wounds to be at maximal swelling and pain. The slightest movement of the wrist, ankles, or trunk would have caused excruciating agony. The most He could have done would have been to hoarsely whisper for help.

The "correct" story should envision that, in this condition, He:

- Unwrapped Himself from within the tight strips of cloth by some undefined mechanism.

- Found the exact spot of the doorway in the darkness of the tomb.

- Somehow, while still inside the tomb, accurately identified the location of the seal which was on the outside and broke it.

- Rolled away the stone (called *golel,* which usually requires multiple strong people to move) all by Himself, from the inside, and did that without making the slightest sound.

- Perfectly timed the breaking of the seal and the rolling away of the stone to those exact moments when every guard was "off duty" at one and the same time.

- Then hobbled off (none of the guards chasing after Him or able to overtake Him) to some location, which, despite the most frantic search, remains unknown to either Jew or Roman to this day.

Have all the questions that naturally arise been satisfactorily explained? Is it easy or difficult to swallow the story that He had only fainted and later had made good His escape by Himself?

Reflecting on the above five points, the most reasonable assertion is that, by the time He was brought down from the cross and laid in the tomb, Christ was dead, with no possibility of escape by Himself.

Theft Theory

1. **The soldier's report: "His disciples came at night and stole him away while we slept"** (Matthew 28:13). This is one explanation for the empty tomb. But the wording of the report shows that it was a false report. One cannot be asleep and awake at the same time. If they were asleep, how did they know it was the *disciples* who stole the body? Their testimony stands discredited. If they were awake, why did they allow the theft? They were the ones armed and stationed there to prevent just this. The report is internally inconsistent. Additionally, the method the disciples used to get into the tomb unnoticed by the posse of professional guards has not yet been outlined. But it does appear to be as improbable as Jesus getting out of the tomb by Himself.

2. **Scene of theft: "The handkerchief . . . folded together in a place by itself"** (John 20:7). Neatness is not a feature of a theft scene. The guards were within striking distance. Haste would have been uppermost in their minds, and disorderliness is the picture to be expected. Or were they meaning to get caught red-handed, while

nonchalantly folding the handkerchief? What could be the explanation for folding clothes!

3. **Naked body: "... Peter ... saw the linen cloths lying by themselves; ..."** (Luke 24:12). This was written during the generation that was witness to the events, but we have no record of anyone disproving it or even challenging this description. If that is the case, we can deduce that the corrected story should say that the disciples carried away a naked body.

   The linen cloths were still in the tomb. Significant questions immediately loom up:

   - What were they hoping to accomplish? The tomb and spices were far more than they could ever think of supplying. In other words, the maximum had already been done to show affection and respect. The most honorable gestures had been made. The body had been tenderly wrapped. They probably knew that the women were preparing special spices to embalm the body. What reason can be given for carrying out a naked body?

   - Why waste time unwrapping the body? It would have made better sense if they had just picked up the wrapped body and bolted. To find a reason for this time-consuming activity, in the face of their intent to steal, is extremely difficult.

   - Crucifixion was reserved for the most despicable criminals. To strip the victims of every last vestige of dignity and heap on them the ultimate expression of shame, they were crucified stark naked. To claim that these disciples stripped their beloved master and carried out His body completely naked, thus heaping insult on that lifeless form, is to meet a psychological hurdle that cannot be crossed in the conservative, eastern parts of the world—where the event actually occurred. No follower of a revered guru will ever even hint of publicly exposing the nakedness of his master. This so-called "correct" story instantly loses credibility.

4. **Soldiers' dereliction: "Therefore command that the tomb be made secure ... lest his disciples ... steal him away ..."** (Matthew 27:64). The soldiers were placed there at the tomb for only one purpose—to see to it that the disciples did not take the body away. To say that every

one of them stopped guarding the tomb at the same time, at the very time when the disciples were at hand, and for the exact length of time required for the disciples to unwrap the body, fold the handkerchief and carry the body to a safe location and out of their jurisdiction, is asking for credulity.

5. **Motive for stealing: "For as yet they did not know the Scripture, that He must rise again from the dead."** (John 20:9.) The disciples did not anticipate the resurrection. Even when the story was brought to them, they were skeptical. **"And their words seemed to them like idle tales, and they did not believe them"** (Luke 24: 10, 11). They had no reason to steal the body. When their leader was arrested but alive, they denied Him and fled out of sheer fright. Is the "correct" story claiming that, after He was tortured to death, the disciples found the courage to rob the body from the tomb, in defiance of the Roman Empire, so that they could proclaim what they knew to be a hoax? The *presence* of the leader usually inspires and motivates. The *death* of the leader is supposed to cause depression, discouragement, and hopelessness. Here, the picture is reversed without an explanation, and that does not make much sense.

Looking over these five points, the suggestion of theft by the disciples seems to strain our sense of reasoning, and at the same time, faces what could be an insurmountable psychological hurdle.

"Non-miraculous explanations of what happened at the empty tomb have to face a cruel choice: either they have to re-write the evidence to suit themselves or they have to accept the fact that they are not consistent with present evidence." Winfried Corduan, *No Doubt About It: The Case for Christianity*, quoted in McDowell, *New Evidence That Demands a Verdict*, p. 257).

The evidence is strongly against the suggestions that Jesus did not die (swoon theory) or that the body was stolen by the disciples (theft theory).

We should be free to inquire about and consider other options.

Evidences for the Written Story

1. After-effects
2. Eyewitnesses
3. Deathbed confessions

After-effects

The change in the disciples.

"Perhaps the transformation of the disciples of Jesus is the greatest evidence of all for the resurrection." J. R. W. Stott, *Basic Christianity* (Downers Grove, IL: Intervarsity Press, 1971), pp. 58, 59.

"A little band of defeated cowards cowering in an upper room one day and a few days later transformed into a company that no persecution could silence" (J. N. D. Anderson, *Christianity Today,* March 29, 1968, pp. 5, 6).

"They were willing to face arrest, imprisonment, beatings and horrible deaths and not one of them. . . recanted of his belief that Christ had risen" (J. Rosscup, class notes, La Mirada, California, Talbot Theological Seminary, 1969).

"Think of the psychological absurdity of . . . attempting to attribute this dramatic change to nothing more convincing than a miserable fabrication they were trying to foist upon the world. That simply wouldn't make sense" (J. N. D. Anderson, *Christianity Today,* March 29, 1968).

What could explain the change in the disciples? If they fled from Jesus when He was alive, what caused them to become this bold after He had died? Lying does not make people bold: truth telling does. Falsehood causes apprehension and fear, especially when aware of the dire consequences of exposure.

Could it be true that, knowing their whole story to be one colossal hoax and knowing where they had buried that dead body, they deliberately extolled a bag of broken bones and rotting flesh as being the "Prince of Life" and did it with such intensity, conviction, and power that 3,000 people, steeped in their own traditions, dropped their lifelong, cherished beliefs *in one day* and decided to follow this man? Was it really that easy to sell the lie? These people had come to Jerusalem for a Jewish festival, and most probably were Jews. They would have known that Jesus had been condemned by the highest religious authority, the Sanhedrin; by the highest civil and judicial authority, Rome; and by the highest universal authority, Jehovah God. Something greater and weightier than these three factors would be necessary to make them decide for Jesus. People were amazed at the courage of the disciples. **". . . when they saw the boldness of Peter and John . . . they marveled"** (Acts 4:13). The only event that could possibly explain this boldness and also answer to the challenge of the three factors is the resurrection.

Some think of the disciples as mere gullible fishermen, who grew all starry-eyed about this charlatan masquerading as the Messiah, and with blind, brutish simplicity carried out whatever was commanded them. If they were so bovine, how did they manage to put together such a complex story, intertwined with such lofty themes and ideals and maintaining a fair level of consistency in the narration, while expertly covering up all their falsehoods in such a manner as to mislead brilliant, analytical minds for over twenty centuries? And if they were so smart as to have accomplished such a feat, how can anyone explain their height of folly in inviting and almost prompting the death sentence, for what they themselves knew to be a complete fabrication? To throw away the deep, basic instinct for self-preservation without proper cause and with such abandonment is a sign of insanity, not intelligence. So neither gullibility nor intelligence is an adequate explanation for the change; however, if the resurrection story was true, neither stupidity nor intelligence would be needed as an explanation. The disciples appeared neither shrewd nor shallow. One inference is still possible—they were truthful.

The presence of the Christian Church

This body is the largest in the world and has been in continuous existence since the start. That start involved eleven disciples (after Judas had gone) who wanted to restore the number back to twelve (the number Jesus originally had). In choosing the twelfth member, two criteria were taken into account. One, the person should have accompanied them all the time. Two, he should be able to bear witness of the resurrection.

> **"Therefore all these men who have accompanied us all the time that the Lord Jesus went in and out among us, beginning from the baptism of John to that day when he was taken up from us, one of these must become witness with us of his resurrection"** (Acts 1:21, 22).

At its inception, when it was nascent and unadorned, the message was not a newfangled "ism," religion or a set of doctrines and teachings. It was the shocking claim that this man had risen from the dead, and as startling and unbelievable as that might have sounded, it was the truth—they were witnesses to it. Therefore, His teachings were to be treated on a different level altogether, because they were backed by an event that was unquestionably supernatural. This was the origin and fountainhead of what is now the global body called the Christian church.

"The resurrection gave significance to all that they did" (L. L. Morris, quoted in McDowell, *New Evidence That Demands a Verdict*, p. 257).

Everything else was to be secondary. Around this pivotal point, every single utterance would revolve. From this nucleus alone would everything else emerge. Without this, they had nothing to proclaim; with this, they appeared invincible. **"Christianity stands or falls with the truth of the resurrection. Once disprove it and you have disposed of Christianity."** Michael Green, *Man Alive*, (Leicester: Intervarsity Press, 1967), p. 61. Throughout the succeeding centuries, despite adding an immense load of baggage, good and bad; despite detractors by the dozen; the Church has remained a real-life entity, the existence of which cannot be disputed. Tracing it back to its origin, only one reasonable cause exists for its birth and survival—the resurrection. **"The institution of the church, then, is a historical phenomenon explained only by Jesus' resurrection"** (McDowell, *New Evidence That Demands a Verdict*, p. 257).

Eyewitnesses

Nobody ever witnessed Gautama Buddha being enlightened under the fichus tree. He made the claim himself. Nobody was present when Muhammad received his many revelations from the angel Gabriel on Mt. Hira. The authors of the Hindu scriptures wrote what was handed down to them. They did not experience the actual stories themselves.

Therefore, it is unique to find an ancient narrative written by one who claimed to have experienced and witnessed the events himself or obtained the information from one who had been there. Today's equivalent might be a sworn affidavit. We may find discrepancies and be tempted to even question the whole document, but the basic story cannot be discarded without being extremely unfair and unreasonable. In which of the ancient writings can we hope to find such unequivocal claims by eyewitnesses? Just look at these affirmations from the New Testament:

- "Those who from the beginning were ***eyewitnesses***" (Luke 1:1-3).
- ". . . but were ***eyewitnesses*** of his majesty" (1 Peter 1:16).
- ". . . he who has ***seen*** has testified" (John 19:35).
- "That which we have ***heard***, which we have ***seen with our eyes***, which we have looked upon and ***our hands have handled***. . ." (1 John 1:1).

- "This Jesus God raised up, of which we are all ***witnesses***." (Acts 2:32).
- ". . . whom God raised from the dead, of which we are ***witnesses***" (Acts 3:15).
- "For we cannot but speak the things which we have ***seen and heard***" (Acts 4:20).
- "Him God raised up on the third day and showed Him openly . . . even to us ***who ate and drank with Him*** after He arose from the dead" (Acts 10: 40, 41).
- "But God raised Him from the dead. He was ***seen*** for many days by those . . . who are His ***witnesses***" (Acts 13:30, 31).
- "After that He was ***seen by over five hundred brethren*** at once, of whom the greater part remain to the present . . ." (1 Corinthians 15:6).

In other words, at that time, it would have been possible to examine and cross-examine actual eyewitnesses. Not only did they give their own testimony, they also appealed to the knowledge of the hearers to substantiate their claim:

"Jesus of Nazareth, a Man attested by God to you by miracles, wonders and signs . . . *as you yourselves also know*. . ." (Acts 2:22, italics supplied). These were the words of Peter to the Jews in Jerusalem.

"Why should it be thought incredible by you that God raises the dead? . . . For the king before whom I also speak freely, *knows these things* . . . since this thing was not done in a corner" (Acts 26:8, 26, italics supplied) This was the claim of Paul before a foreign king, King Agrippa, and it was not refuted by the king. To openly appeal to those who are not exactly friendly is quite risky, unless the facts are incontrovertible.

How impartial and even-handed would it be simply to toss these statements away, without demonstrating deception or falsehood?

These are significant words and especially remarkable, coming from a very ancient period when eyewitness accounts were rare. We should be able to give them the weight they deserve. Further, how much more data should anyone require before considering the story a possibility?

> **"The very kind of evidence which modern science—and even psychologists, are so insistent upon for determining the reality of any object under consideration is the kind of evidence that we have presented to us in the Gospels regarding the resurrection of the Lord**

Jesus, namely, the things that are seen with the human eye, touched with the human hand and heard with the human ear. This is what we call *empirical evidence*" (Smith, *Therefore Stand*, pp. 389, 390). A written statement by an eyewitness is one of the strongest evidences to be tabled in a court of law today. Such appears to be the story in the New Testament.

Deathbed Confessions

Generally accepted is the reality that somewhere in the back of most minds, even when not explicitly confessed, is the fearful notion of a coming cosmic judgment. Hardened criminals, at the point of death, are known to soften up and become truthful, rather than stand the thought of condemnation on that dreadful "day of reckoning." This, simply put, is the basis of accepting a death-bed confession as the truth. Rarely is such a confession dismissed as falsehood, when uttered while facing the specter of death.

A death-bed confession from an eyewitness is a powerful form of judicial evidence. If two or three death-bed confessions from eyewitnesses tell the same basic story, the chances of it being nullified by a jury in a court of law are very slim indeed. The resurrection report is *founded* on deathbed confessions.

> **"They were willing to face arrest, imprisonment, beatings and horrible deaths and not one of them . . . recanted of his belief that Christ had risen"** (J. Rosscup, quoted in McDowell, *New Evidence That Demands a Verdict* [hereinafter abbreviated as NEDV], p. 270.).

Tradition has it that:

- Peter was crucified upside down.
- James was stoned to death.
- Matthew was killed by the sword.
- James (son of Alpheus) was crucified.
- James (son of Zebedee) was killed by the sword.
- Thaddaeus was shot through with arrows.
- Bartholomew was crucified.
- Philip was crucified.
- Simon the Zealot was crucified.

- Thomas was killed with the spear.
- Paul was beheaded.

(Muncaster, *A Skeptic's Search for God*, p. 203).

These were not slaughtered together but were sentenced to death, one at a time, over years and decades.

Ample opportunity was available for them to reconsider the reasons for their stand. How tempting would have been the thought of confessing the "truth," regaining their former position in society, and returning to the peace and pleasure of their homes and families, if it was all a hoax. Why such horrendous deaths, for no cause at all? Imagine dying for "Alice," who promised a life in "Wonderland"! That would not stand to reason. One might die for what was *taken* to be truth, but not for what was *known* to be fanciful make-believe.

Multiple death-bed confessions of the same basic story by eyewitnesses cannot be overturned by any fair and just jury.

> **"Indeed taking all the evidence together, it is not too much to say that there is no historic incident better or more variously supported than the resurrection of Christ"** (B. F. Westcott, quoted by Paul Little, *Know Why You Believe*, 1987).

> **"On that greatest point we are not merely asked to have faith. In its favor as living truth, there exists such overwhelming evidence, positive and negative, factual and circumstantial, that no intelligent jury in the world could fail to bring in a verdict that the resurrection story is true"** (Lord Darling, Chief Justice of England, quoted by Michael Green, *Man Alive*, pp. 53, 54).

> **"Thousands and tens of thousands of persons have gone through it piece by piece as carefully as every judge summing up a most important case. I have myself done it many times over, not to persuade others but to satisfy myself . . . and I know of no one fact in the history of mankind which is proved by better and fuller evidence of every sort, to the understanding of a fair inquirer, than that Christ died and rose again from the dead"** (Thomas Arnold, Chairman of the Department of Modern History, Oxford University, quoted by Wilbur Smith, *Therefore Stand*, pp. 425, 426).

Arnold Toynbee studied people who called themselves "savior" in various times and places. In *A study of History*, vol. 6, p. 276, he sums it up thusly:

"When we set out on this quest we found ourselves moving in the midst of a mighty marching host... In the last stage of all, our motley host of would-be saviours, human and divine, has dwindled to a single company of none but gods . . . At the final ordeal of death, few, even of these would-be saviour-gods, have dared to put their title to the test by plunging into the icy river. And now as we stand and gaze with our eyes fixed upon the farther shore, a single figure rises from the flood and straightway fills the whole horizon. There is the Saviour."

"The bones of Abraham, and Muhammad and Buddha and Confucius and Lao Tzu and Zoroaster are still here on earth. Jesus' tomb is empty. It is the concrete, factual, empirical proof that: life has hope and meaning; love is stronger than death; goodness and power are ultimately allies, not enemies; life wins in the end; God has touched us right here where we are and has defeated our last enemy; we are not cosmic orphans . . ." Peter Kreeft and Ronald Tacelli, *Handbook of Christian Apologetics* (Downers Grove, IL: InterVarsity Press, 1994), p. 177.

The inquiring mind must bow to the weight of evidence.

Conclusion

Let us summarize the ten points we have considered and deliberated:

1. The New Testament is the best-documented ancient writing in the world, and it is solidly historical in nature. Despite the scientifically unexplained events recorded, it should not be dismissed as legendary or mythological but examined in a fair manner.

2. The top feature of the Judeo-Christian Scripture—cross-referencing of other authors separated by centuries and thus claiming a supervisor who lived the whole period of at least 1,400 years—is impressive and has characteristics that are beyond human capability.

3. The Bible's challenge to test it for authenticity is open and clear—the only Scripture with this distinction. And it fulfills its own challenge, predictive prophecy, with amazing accuracy.

   These three factors place the writing at the highest level of credibility that any ancient document can hope to reach.

4. Jesus dared to make the highest claim for Himself—Son of God. Because He does not fit into the description of a raving lunatic, an incorrigible liar, or a pompous egomaniac, the claim remains a possibility.

5. Jesus did not just explain and expound the truth, the way, and the life but claimed to be the very essence of them. "I *am* the way, the truth and the life," He said.

6. Jesus is the only founder (the only known person on earth) in whom the theory of teaching was matched by actual practice in life—therefore, the only one with the right to say, "Follow Me."

7. Jesus is the only founder to be of questionable birth and mocked as "illegitimate." Yet that epithet could bring in the possibility of His Father being out of this world.

8. Jesus' ministry was by far the shortest, compared to any other founder, yet it has had the greatest impact.

9. Jesus is the only founder to die the shameful, violent death of a condemned criminal. This raises a slew of questions regarding the devotion granted Him by the hundreds of millions, even thousands of years later. A criminal managing to split civilized history in two—B.C. and A.D.—must be no ordinary criminal.

10. Jesus is the only founder to go into the domain of death, the most feared enemy of mankind, break its bands, and come back as a Conqueror over death. And He now claims to offer eternal life to "whosoever believes" in Him.

The last seven features point to an incomparable claim regarding this man.

Taking all ten together, they form a combination that reaches an uncommon mark. Do they constitute absolute proof? No, they don't. I myself can raise questions that cannot be answered. But if I should toss out the whole, it would not serve the purpose of the search. I was looking for something to go by, and I found this to be the best. I cannot imagine another claim backed by such an array of solid, open, testable points of evidence. The credibility is of the highest order possible; however, if there is another claim of greater veracity and credibility, I would like to know so I can consider that, too. But until such time, will you, dear reader, grant me your full and honest permission to follow this man written about in this book?

No, I do not demand that you agree. All I ask is that you carefully weigh the evidence and then think, "This person (me) does have a justifiable ground to stand on. His belief does appear reasonable and evidence-based." And once you've said that, then let me challenge you to "Go and find *your* reason to believe."

And may the God of Truth guide you and bring you safely to the harbor of fulfillment and meaning in your life.

What a journey we've had together! What say we meet again?

Section II

The Sequel

Introduction

Some unfinished tasks were left over from my previous discussion in Section I. Not the pressing kind, they persisted in the shadows nonetheless, nudging my inquiring spirit just enough to keep me on the road. I knew I would have to consider and address them as part of my search. Only then could I rest with a good sense of culmination to it: hence, this sequel.

In the course of looking at the various factors used for comparison, I had deliberately laid a few aside. These included claims that were insisted on as unique by a particular religion, but on a closer view, they were not, because other religions also had made similar claims. Since they were not really unique, I had felt that they would not help in making a decision regarding the "Only Way" and were not given any place in that discussion. However, they were obviously very important—important enough to be placed in the forefront as a distinctive feature of that religion. I found twelve such claims. Would something of worth come out of examining those non-unique, albeit important claims?

The final picture in Section One pointed to Jesus and the Bible as possessing features of immense credibility. The conclusions drawn appeared fairly strong. But were they just an incidental, random list of features, or was there some pattern to them, such as maybe a sequence suggesting an internal consistency of thought?

What about the Man and the Book? Did they have qualities that not only caused them to differ from the others but were also attractive in themselves? Would they still retain their charm and appeal? Would they remain credible and impressive enough to engender homage, even when the focus was not a comparison?

The titles given the various sacred writings were meant to convey a certain thought or idea regarding the contents of the book. The Mahabharata of the Hindus means "Great Narrative." The context of the message is an epic. One of the Buddhist volumes is called "Tibetan Book of the Dead," which is a description of the forty-nine days that bridges between the end of one form of existence and the beginning of the next. The Quran of the Muslims is a "Recitation." Muhammad recited the words that the angel Gabriel gave him (because he could neither read nor write himself). The Judaic writings are described as the "Law and the Prophets." They contain moral and ethical codes and a plethora of messages from those claiming to be God's spokesmen. The Christian message of the New Testament is based on the story of Jesus and is called the *Gospel*, which means "good news." Why was this word chosen? Is there more to it than meets the eye? The study unravels a basic premise of the faith.

Some of the questions at the end of chapter 11 of Section One were addressed in chapter 12. However, one significant question lingered. Jesus was seen to be the most innocent, His life acknowledged as the most blameless, yet He died the most horrible death. It can be accepted, and indeed has been documented, that human systems of justice can sometimes go bad—very bad. But should that be said of "cosmic," ultimate justice? Did divine, perfect fairness and equity go awry? Who was responsible for this terrifying injustice? The probe takes us to the very heart of the claims of Christianity.

In this real-life drama, everybody is part of the original cast. Nobody has been left out. Nobody is a mere spectator. Nobody is unimportant. Whether on center stage or behind the scenes, whether in the glare of the limelight or in the shadowy periphery, whether approved or ridiculed, everyone's role is going to count in the final analysis. If that is the case, what is my part? Is this a tragedy, a comedy, a spectacular extravaganza, or a one-of-a-kind, unpredictable combination? Are we in mid-play, or is this an interlude? What about the finale?

Who's got the script? How should I respond?

Wow! The questions—so many of them. Is anyone out there claiming to know and provide all the answers? I don't know for sure, but if possible answers are anywhere, I can't see them falling into the lap of a slacker snoozing in a hammock. A chance exists, if we are going to be deliberate and diligent. So . . .

COME—LET'S SEARCH AGAIN.

13

Non-Unique Factors

The natural temptation to portray what we espouse in the most attractive light often leads to statements that are not entirely true. Enthusiastic followers have made claims that, at first glance, seem impressive but, on scrutiny, are found to be exaggerations. One such type is the claim that a certain feature is unique to a religion. In other words, the feature is so special and distinctive that no other religion can equal it. During my search, these quickly grabbed my attention and, many times, made quite an impact. But since I was doing a comparison, I looked over what others also were saying. At that point, the specific claim of uniqueness lost credibility, because the other religions also displayed similar characteristics. They could not be retained as unique. The following are twelve such claims:

1. A Complete Message

This claim states that the message contained in their writings covers all the facets of life. The introduction to the Quran, IFTA Call and Guidance, under the heading "Unique Factors," claims that it **"contains a complete code which provides for all areas of life, whether spiritual, intellectual, political, social or economic."** The Muslim contention is that the Quran is the only book that contains such a spectrum of admonitions. But even a cursory reading of the Christian, Hindu, and Buddhist literature will show them not only to supply these but to do so in greater measure and greater detail. Definitely, they are described in a more systematic manner and, therefore, in clearer terms. The Vedas of the Hindus, the books of Exodus and Leviticus in the Bible, and the Pratimoksha rules of the Buddhists are excellent examples of these.

2. Faith and Love Are Dominant

Christians like to claim that their religion involves faith and love, while the others rely only on performance of good deeds. This may appear true, but it is not wholly so.

a. **Hinduism: "Those who . . . are always engaged in worshiping Me with great and transcendental *faith* are considered by Me to be most perfect"** (Bhagavad-Gita, 12:2, italics supplied).

   "Those who . . . completely engage themselves with faith, making Me the supreme goal are very, very dear to Me" (Bhagavad-Gita, 12:20, italics supplied).

b. **Buddhism: ". . . the path to salvation lies not in the performance of good works but in a life of *faith* and devotion to the Buddha Amitabh"** (Chen, *Buddhism the Light of Asia,* italics supplied).

c. **Islam: "As for those that have *faith* and do good works—they shall forever dwell in the gardens of paradise . . ."** (The Quran, 18:107, italics supplied).

   "Proclaim good tidings to those who have faith and do good works" (The Quran, 2:25).

d. **Christianity: "He who hears My word and believes in Him who sent Me has everlasting life . . . has passed from death to life"** (John 5:24).

In fairness, it should be pointed out that while faith is spoken of, it is the inexorable law of "karma," that veritably dominates and permeates Hindu and Buddhist thought.

3. God the Savior

Portrayed as a predominant feature of Christianity, this concept is not an emphasis in the others, but this picture is certainly depicted in them, too

a. **Hinduism:** The various avatars of Vishnu were for the express purpose of saving mankind. The first avatar was Matsya the Fish, who saved Manu the progenitor of the human race from a devastating flood brought into the world by the wickedness in it.

b. **Buddhism: ". . . He (Amitabh, a Bodhisatva) vowed that anyone who has faith in him as the savior will be re-born in that Pure Land . . . his faithful assistant bodhisattva Avalokiteshwara . . . is described as being ever ready to come down to earth to lead the faithful . . . to salvation. . ."** (Chen, *Buddhism the Light of Asia*, p. 70).

c. **Christianity: "For the Son of Man has come to save that which was lost"** (Matthew 18:11).

   This concept is absent in Islam, and even though it is present in Hinduism and Buddhism, the evaluation and judgment of a life is still based primarily on the performances of meritorious deeds by the individual.

4. Incarnation, Savior-God

a. **Hinduism:** The avatars came to help humans see the correct picture and follow the ideals exemplified. Nine such forms of Vishnu have been advanced, with Rama and Krishna (the seventh and eighth) being the most well-known. The tenth is yet to come.

b. **Christianity**: Jesus, the Incarnate, came to bear the load Himself. He did it most visibly on the cross on Calvary.

c. **Buddhism**: The early Theravada form did not describe this concept, but the later Mahayana literature described Gautama Buddha as the Emanation form of the Supreme Buddha known as Adi-buddha. **"This eternal Buddha became incarnated as Sakyamuni, the son of Maya"** (Chen, *Buddhism the Light of Asia*, p. 65).

This concept is absent in Islam and is still in the future in Judaism. In Hinduism, the avatars came primarily to show and to teach. The salvation of the individual still rested mainly on the performance of requirements—on good deeds, or "karma."

5. One Supreme Being

a. **Islam**, with some justification, can possibly claim this as unique. However, a closer look at the other religions shows an interesting discovery—that in the ultimate sense, there is but one Supreme Being in the other religions too.

b. **Hinduism:** Here, the Supreme Being is the ultimate Eternal Brahman, who forms the universe with a fraction of himself. All the so-called pantheon of gods, goddesses, and demi-gods are but different forms or emanations from a Primeval Body.

c. **Buddhism:** In Mahayana **Buddhism** there are many Buddhas, but they are all manifestations of the Triple Body of the Eternal Buddha. **"The eternal Buddha creates a fictitious phantom of himself and causes this to appear among ignorant and wicked mankind in order to convert it. Sakyamuni was such a phantom"** (Chen, p. 66). (Sakyamuni is one of the names for Gautama Buddha.)

d. **Judaism**: **"Hear O Israel: The Lord our God, the Lord is one"** (Deuteronomy 6:4).

e. **Christianity**: Although there is the concept of the Trinity, the essence of "God" is only one and is described in the singular. **"One Lord, one faith, one baptism"** (Ephesians 4:5).

Visible differences exist, but the claim of "One Supreme Being" is not unique.

6. Revealed, Not Man-Made

a. **Buddha** was "enlightened" under the tree in Bodhgaya. ". . . and his words are not those of a mere man, but a voice issuing from another world" (Conze, *Buddhist Scriptures*, p. 14).

b. **Moses** was "given" the commandments, statutes, and judgments. **"I [Moses] stood between the Lord and you at that time, to declare to you the word of God"** (Deuteronomy 5:5). **"These words the Lord spoke to all your assembly in the mountain from the midst of the fire, the cloud and the thick darkness . . ."** (Deuteronomy 5:22).

c. **Muhammad** was "spoken to" by the angel Gabriel. **"This book is beyond all doubt revealed by the Lord of the Universe"** (The Quran, 32:1).

d. **Hinduism**: **"Lord Krishna said, 'I instructed this imperishable science of yoga to the Sun-god Vivasvan and Vivasvan instructed it to Manu, the father of mankind'"** (Bhagavad-Gita, 4:1).

e. **Christianity**: **". . . prophecy never came by the will of man but holy men of God spoke as they were moved by the Holy Spirit"** (2 Peter 1:21). **"All scripture is given by inspiration of God . . ."** (2 Timothy 3:16).

All the scriptures claim this as being true.

7. Beyond Reason and Logic

This claim is held not only as unique but is also as the reason why a particular religion cannot be brought to scrutiny—it is a major premise of Buddhism and Hinduism. But all religions, at some point, appeal to truths being beyond our ability to fathom.

a. **Islam: "I (Allah) know what you know not . . . I know the secrets of the heavens and the earth . . ."** (The Quran, 2:32, 33).

b. **Judaism: "For My thoughts are not your thoughts, nor are your ways My ways. For as the heavens are higher than the earth, so are My ways higher than your ways, and My thoughts than your thoughts"** (Isaiah 55:8, 9).

c. **Hinduism: "Krishna descends to this planet once in a day of Brahma, or every 8,600,000,000 years . . . we have to accept it as it is, otherwise there is no point in trying to understand the Bhagavad-Gita and its speaker Lord Krishna"** (Bhagavad-Gita, Preface, p. xix).

d. **Christianity**: **"Eye has not seen, nor ear heard, nor have entered into the heart of man, the things which God has prepared for those who love Him"** (1 Corinthians 2:9).

8. Experience of Blessings in Present Life

This claim sought to refute the common taunt that religious concepts and promises only float up there in the clouds without ever actually touching the ground. The ideas are so focused on the "other world" that they are of no relevance to life here on earth. So each claimant wanted to show that the present life was not being ignored. The notion was worth promoting, but it was not unique to any one of the religions.

a. **Hinduism: " . . . The self-realized person enjoys unlimited happiness. . ."** (Bhagavad-Gita, 5:21).

   "Those situated in that mode become conditioned by a sense of happiness. . ." (Bhagavad-Gita, 14:6).

b. **Islam: " . . . To those that embrace the Faith ... We will surely grant a happy life"** (The Quran, 16:96). **"That which is revealed in the Quran is a balm and blessing to true believers"** (The Quran 17:82).

c. **Judaism: "Blessed shall be the fruit of your body, the produce of your ground and the increase of your herds . . ."** (Deuteronomy 28:4).

d. **Christianity: "And everyone who has left . . . houses or . . . lands . . . for My name's sake, shall receive a hundredfold in this life..., and inherit eternal life"** (Mark 10:30).

9. Experience the Key

The foremost proponents of this idea are **Hinduism** and **Buddhism**. The reliance is on a supposedly mystical experience so enchanting and unique that it settles the question of authenticity and credibility regarding the claim. The plea is that the reality of the religion can only be "tasted" and not questioned from the "outside." So it has to be accepted as such. The very fact that there are two claimants suggests that it is not unique.

a. **Islam: "This Book is not to be doubted. It is a guide for the righteous . . . who believe in what has been revealed to you . . ."** (The Quran, 2:1).

b. **Hinduism**: **". . . should at least theoretically accept Sri Krishna as the Supreme Personality of the Godhead . . ."** (Bhagavad-Gita, Introduction, p. 7).

c. **Christianity**: **"My peace I give to you; not as the world gives do I give to you"** (John 14:27); **"... and the peace of God, which surpasses all understanding, will guard your hearts and minds . . ."** (Philippians 4:7).

d. **Judaism: "O taste and see that the Lord is good"** (Psalm 34:8).

10. Universal Application

This claim attempts to downplay the exclusive nature of beliefs. The inclusive picture is placed in the forefront by Hinduism and Buddhism, but on examining the other religions, a universal application is found in those claims, too.

a. **Buddhism: "He is indeed a teacher for all mankind of *all* ages"** (Chen, p. 29).

b. **Hinduism: "Lord Krishna declares, I am the Father of *all*"** (Bhagavad-Gita, p. 17). **". . . It is possible for us to see that Sanatana Dharma is the business of all the people of the world . . ."** (p. 18).

c. **Judaism: "Have *all* we not all *one* Father? Has not God created us?"** (Malachi 2:10). **"Also the sons of a stranger . . . will I bring to My holy mountain . . . for My house shall be called a house of prayer for *all* nations"** (Isaiah 56:7).

d. **Christianity: "That was the true Light which gives light to *every* Man . . ."** (John 1:9). **"Is He the God of Jews only? Is He not also the God of the Gentiles? Yes, of the Gentiles also . . ."** (Romans 3:29). **"And He Himself is the propitiation for our sins, and not for ours only but also for the *whole world*"** (1 John 2:2).

11. Presence of Miracles

The particular miracles are presented as unique features. In a sense, they are unique, but that does not in itself suggest that the religion be placed on a pedestal. Other religions may not have had the same miracle, but they certainly claimed to have their own. So the presence of miracles itself was not actually unique. Numerous examples of these amazing stories are available. Here are just a few:

a. **Islam:** When Muhammad was born, milk began to flow in copious amounts from the one nursing him and also from the camel that belonged to them.

b. **Buddhism**: Buddha was able to speak the moment he was born. He declared his mission of enlightenment and then took seven steps, with a lotus flower growing out of the ground at each step.

c. **Hinduism**: Krishna had miraculous powers of strength and transportation and an incredible ability in archery—an ability to shoot multiple arrows for prolonged lengths of time.

d. **Judaism:** Some examples of miracles in Judaism include the following: The crossing of the Red Sea and the River Jordan, the falling of the walls of Jericho, the raising of the dead by Elijah, and prophetic visions into distant futures.

e. **Christianity**: Examples of miracles include healing of various diseases, feeding thousands from only one meal, walking on water, calming a violent storm with just a verbal command, and raising the dead to live again.

12. Surpassing Worth of the Goal

The attempt of each religion was to make it so attractive that nobody in his right mind would think of discarding the offer. The descriptions were of exquisite beauty and of transcendent worth. Each was portraying something rare and special and, therefore, claiming uniqueness, but the others, too, had similar claims.

a. **Islam: ". . . God will admit them to gardens watered by running streams. They shall be decked with bracelets of gold and of pearls and arrayed in garments of silk"** (The Quran, 22:21-23).

". . . feasting on fruit and honoured in the gardens of delight. Reclining face to face upon soft couches, they shall be served with a goblet filled at the gushing fountain. . . . They shall sit with bashful, dark-eyed virgins, as chaste as the sheltered eggs of ostriches" (Ibid., 37:39).

"You shall be served with golden dishes and golden cups. . . . You shall find all that your souls desire and all that your eyes rejoice in" (Ibid., 43:70).

b. **Hinduism**: **"Purified of sinful reactions, they take birth on the pious heavenly planet of Indra, where they enjoy godly delights"** (Bhagavad-Gita, 9:20). **"That supreme abode of mine. . . . Those who reach it never return to this material world"** (Ibid., 15:6).

c. **Buddhism: " . . . Western Paradise which is described as being fertile, comfortable ... It is adorned with fragrant trees and flowers, and decorated with the most beautiful jewels and gems. Rivers with scented waters give forth musical sounds and are flanked on both**

sides with scented jewelled trees. . . . Nowhere does one meet with anything unpleasant . . ." (Chen, p. 70).

d. **Christianity: "And God shall wipe away every tear from their eyes; there shall be no more death, nor sorrow, nor crying. There shall be no more pain . . ."** (Revelation 21:4).

"The twelve gates were twelve pearls . . . and the street of the city was pure gold like transparent glass" (Ibid., 21:21). **" . . . On either side of the river was the tree of life, which bore twelve fruits, each tree yielding its fruit every month. . . . And there shall be no more curse . . ."** (Ibid., 22:2, 3).

Taken together, the list contains impressive features indeed. The five religions had given great importance to each of these points, displaying them as such marks of distinction that they would undoubtedly sway anyone into their camp. If ever there was a set of beliefs/claims that could be used to form a generic religion that would appeal to all the proponents of these different faiths, this was it.

So I formed that set—that "religion"—then pitted the claims of each of the different religions against this list. Amazingly, Christianity alone answered to that generic religion. It had all twelve features among its claims. And these claims were not just glancing references but direct, forthright utterances placing them at the fundamental level of its "stock in trade." No other religion could match this spectrum.

What a source from which to retrieve credibility—a list I had earlier discarded and set aside as unhelpful in my search for the "Only Way"! But here it was—evidence difficult to deny or refute.

A religion whose clear, specific claims are found to cover the spectrum of factors declared to be important to all five major world religions must be classified as genuinely unique.

14

Conclusions of the Search

Ten conclusions were reached in Section One. They seem naturally to fall into sets of three points each. The first set describes the characteristics of the writings. The second shows the founder in the best light possible, and the third draws a pitiful picture and places Him at the bottom. Here they are:

1. The New Testament is the best-documented ancient writing in the world and is solidly historical in nature.
2. The top feature of the Judeo-Christian scripture—cross-referencing of authors separated by centuries—is impressive and has characteristics that are beyond human capability.
3. The Bible's challenge to test it for authenticity is open and clear—the only scripture with this distinction.
4. Jesus dared to make the highest claim for himself—Son of God.
5. Jesus claimed not just to bring a message but to *be* the message. He said, "I *am* the Truth."
6. Jesus is the only Founder in whom the theory of teaching was perfectly matched by actual practice in life.
7. Jesus is the only Founder to be of questionable birth and mocked as "illegitimate."
8. The ministry of Jesus was, by far, the shortest compared to that of the other founders.
9. Jesus is the only Founder to die the shameful, violent death of a condemned criminal.
10. He is the only one to go into the domain of death, break its bands and come back as a Conqueror over death.

The Writings

The New Testament has the best bibliographical basis of any religious text in all of ancient history. Nothing in ancient literature can match such textual integrity. In other words, nobody should ever treat it as being on the same plane as a myth or a legend, because the characteristics that define such types of literature are just not present.

If we acknowledge that at times, "truth is stranger than fiction," then the fair attitude should lead us to calmly examine, rather than to dismiss with disdain. This "best attestation" is not in comparison only to other religious writings but includes the entire spectrum of ancient literature—the Sumerian, the Mayan, the Babylonian, the Egyptian, the Phoenician, the Chinese, the Indian, the Greek, the Roman, and all others. It stands first among *all* ancient writings, as solidly historical in nature. If it is to be challenged and set aside on this point, every other ancient writing should be held on an inferior level, and we should question all that we have claimed to know of ancient history on Planet Earth.

The literature was written over a period of about 1,400 years. The authors claimed that the messages came from one single source—the "Lord." The "Lord" supervised the writing of the various portions of the Bible for these 1,400 years. Nobody can live that long, nor can they have such a vast influence over people from so many backgrounds and walks of life, compelling them to write on a single topic. This feat is definitely beyond human capability.

Also, it was the only literature that invited and actually summoned the inquirer to test it out on the level of verifiable data that was not specifically religious in nature. The string of prophecies, which formed the basis of this test, dealt with events that were not the kind that only a religious interpretation could decipher and unravel. These included such things as victories and defeats in battle, the setting up of a sequence of world empires, a specific amount of money, the place of a birth, the method of an execution, specific activities of some foreign soldiers at the site of execution, and precise descriptions such as bones being intact but joints dislocated. These can be reasonably tested and verified.

The magnitude of this claim is astounding—ten or a dozen of them would have been enough to astonish and render one spellbound, but there are *hundreds* of such prophecies that were made and accurately fulfilled. No other religious writing or leader made such predictions which were ultimately shown to be true. To simply cast doubt without refuting the evidence is to portray an attitude that is predeterministic and, therefore, biased. The information we have from historical records and from archeology makes this challenge practically irrefutable.

So, here's the picture regarding the Judeo-Christian Scriptures: Among all ancient literature, it is the best attested and, therefore, to be taken as unquestionably historical in nature. This, in itself, should have been sufficient to draw admiration and attention. But more, it then displays a feature that is impossible for any human to attain. Adding to these, it is the only scripture to extend a universal challenge to test it for authenticity. This portrays an impressive degree of confidence in the credibility of the material being presented and constitutes a rare set, indeed. While each of the points is impressive in itself, they are not disconnected and unrelated but form a combination in which each builds upon the other. This is what makes the Book truly unbeatable.

Turning now to the Founder, Jesus of Nazareth . . .

The Positive Picture

The three features here are regarding

- Christ's claim to be God
- His claim to be the message and the truth
- The record of an unblemished life

The first is an absolutely stunning claim—to be the Son of God. In other words, He claimed to have come from another dimension—the dimension where absolute truth resides. If that was the case, and if He came down to us incarnated as a human, that human should have the truth inherent in Himself. That is, indeed, what we find in His claim to not only bring the message but to *be* the message. He did not feel compelled to go looking for it, as did Buddha, who was relentless in his search, or Muhammad, who was allowed some rare communications from the angel Gabriel on Mt. Hira. His was a simple, clear-cut claim—**"I am the Truth!"** And if He was the Truth, then His whole life should have been in line with, and permeated by, that truth. No deviation from the standard should have been evident—and no sin requiring forgiveness. That is precisely the record we have of His life—**"In Him there is no sin"** (1 John 3:5); **"without blemish, without spot"** (1 Peter 1:19). **"Sinless perfection and perfect sinlessness is what we would expect of God-incarnate, and this we find in Jesus Christ. The hypothesis and facts concur."** Bernard Ramm, *Protestant Christian Evidences* (Chicago, IL: Moody Press, 1957), p. 169. This last point is more than a claim—it is a testimony that was endorsed by a wide spectrum of the society of His day.

As such, it becomes a reasonable basis for the first two points. **"Jesus led the one perfect life of piety and personal holiness on the sole consideration that He was God incarnate"** (Ramm, Ibid.). These three factors form a chain linked together in an amazing, consistent manner. The harmony and progression appear compelling.

The Negative Side

But the next three—a) His illegitimate birth, b) His ultra-short period of ministry, and c) His death as a cursed criminal—pull Him down from that pedestal and show Him in the worst light possible. His was the worst start in life, the shortest period of ministry, and the most disgraceful ending—that of a vile felon, from whose lips was wrung that bitter expression of being forsaken by God Himself. This set, with each gloomy feature progressively worse, forms the most pitiable picture of any life imaginable. How could anyone have started a moral, ethical revolution from such a dismal base? It had the word *IMPOSSIBLE* stamped all over it! His name should have been buried in the ashes of utter ruin and failure in the very next generation. No simple, logical explanation exists for what we see as a vast, thriving movement today.

So one set places Him at the highest spot possible, while the other forces Him to murky depths. However, these very extremes are significant. In the early part of the search, one of the factors pointing to the "Only Way" was not just of being ahead but, more important, of being different from the others.

These six points, taken together, seem to establish just that. When He is "good," He's at the top, and when He's discredited, He's at the tail-end or out of sight! He appears always different, always by Himself, always in a different class.

The story does not end there. Amazingly, there is a claim that goes beyond the grave. That claim is the tenth one, and with that, He irrevocably separates Himself from every other founder. The resurrection claim is a declaration of power over death—a claim nobody else on earth has ever made, or for which anyone has provided evidence. This claim is also the clearest assertion of His right to divinity, and it is on this "Rock" that the Christian Church has laid its foundation and on which it now stands. And all this is recorded in an ancient piece of literature that is neither mythological nor legendary.

Christianity is a sphinx that rose from those very ashes marked "IMPOSSIBLE" and then grew to the colossus that it is. The base is founded squarely on the stunning event at the tomb—the resurrection. The background of impossibility establishes the whole phenomenon as miraculous. Yes, Christianity claims to be a miracle, and every true follower of this Man is the outworking of the miraculous. This was the claim two thousand years ago. The claim remains the same today.

15

The Man

Jesus is not one of the group of the world's great. Talk about Alexander the Great and Charles the Great and Napoleon the Great if you will. . . . Jesus is apart. He is not the Great; He is the Only" (Carnegie Simpson, quoted in NEDV, p. 316).

"I know men and I tell you that Jesus Christ is no mere man. Between Him and every other person in the world there is no possible term of comparison" (Napoleon Bonaparte, quoted in NEDV, p. 317).

Did the authors really mean what they said? Why did they portray Him in such language, as if driven to such conclusions? Why did they use such extreme expressions to pay compliment to One who is supposed to have been an ordinary peasant who died as a condemned criminal? I think there could be many reasons—maybe just to make a splash and get people's attention, maybe to project one's self as a Christian champion, maybe to make some money off of some gullible followers, or maybe to appease a guilty conscience, as examples. All of these have a touch of pretense. Haven't we seen many make a loud profession which then turns out to be mere hypocrisy?

But, what if these persons really meant it? What if it came from a compulsion so strong that these extraordinary words were all they could find to express themselves, because they saw something that brought sheer wonder to their senses? What then?

The most reasonable approach is to look for features that they might have come across. I think there are aspects regarding the life of Jesus that could have possibly evoked such a response.

Here are seven that, taken together, might be cause for marvel and amazement:

1. Unique birth
2. Sinless perfection
3. Impressive words/sayings
4. Miracles
5. Lasting influence
6. Addressed deep needs
7. Conquered death

1. Unique Birth the Entry Point

Here's the claim: this Being—God, in essence—who existed from eternity (**"from everlasting,"** according to Micah 5:2), limited Himself to the form of a human and came to be born of a woman—a virgin. While the story is recorded in the Gospels written during the first century A.D., it was predicted about 600 years earlier by Isaiah, who said that the virgin birth would be a specific sign. The word he used could also be interpreted to mean just a young maiden, and not specifically a virgin, but how then could that have constituted a sign or a marker? How reasonable would it be to tell people to watch out for a green tree, when every tree in sight is green? It would serve the purpose of identification much better to choose an unusual color, such as purple or blue. The words of Isaiah read, **"The Lord Himself will give you a sign . . ."** (Isaiah 7:14). This was to be a *sign* from a supernatural dimension—God Himself. A young maiden becoming pregnant in the normal course of events would hardly have been counted as such a sign—it had to be very, very unusual.

The virgin birth, while an extremely common expression, is an extremely astonishing event. The familiarity of the phrase tends to downplay the startling nature of the claim. We unwittingly relegate it to the level of a myth. It seems too unreal and unbelievable to have actually happened—and, after all, how many religious writings have all kinds of bizarre and fanciful accounts? This is taken to be one of them. So we gloss over it, neither truly believing it nor completely discarding it.

Of course, the Gospel writers could have been familiar with the prediction and described the birth to fit the prophecy. The other side of the coin is no less relevant—they could have told the truth. That aside, there is another basic question: Why would Isaiah have made such a prophecy in the first place? He was a revered prophet in his day. Putting ourselves in his shoes, would we be able to come up with a good reason for this physiologically ridiculous prediction? I wonder if the method of its fulfillment ever crossed his mind. He did not even know when it would come to pass. If it happened in his lifetime, there could have been an insinuation that he planned the hoax and set it up from some ulterior motive. But today, we know from the Dead Sea Scrolls that it was written down hundreds of years before the event. Why would he take the risk of being lampooned as a lunatic for describing such an oddity? No human explanation can reasonably account for this prediction, let alone its fulfillment.

Looking down through history, only one serious claim has been advanced as the fulfillment—the birth of Jesus. While no one can say that it definitely took place, nobody can claim the opposite, either—that it definitely did not happen. Refuting the claim of the virgin birth might have been possible, had both parents of Jesus been identified. Here is precisely where it becomes interesting, because in the Gospels, as well as in the traditional writings of the Jews (who did not accept Jesus as Messiah and treated Him as if He were any other human), Jesus is called illegitimate.

Everybody knew who His mother was, but the paternal side was in question, because no one was able to identify the father. In this setting, the nativity account and claim of the Gospel writers—that the "father" was God—still stands as a possibility. Obviously, the whole story would have to be a miraculous one, with the virgin birth as part of that miracle. It is reasonable then, to make an assertion that this was the "sign" prophesied—something so out of the ordinary that it could not be duplicated. The account in the Gospels may yet be the truth—the fact of the matter.

Taking it at face value, it can be said that the virgin birth story is an absolutely unique account of God's entry into time and space, and thus into human history. We look in vain for a comparable story, apart from mythological accounts. (The New Testament does not seem to fit the description of a myth—see chapter 3 of Section One.) What an unusual start to a biography!

2. Sinless Perfection

I have stood amazed many times in the contemplation of this aspect of Christ's life. How would I have felt if I could look into those dark recesses of my private life and desires, to find everything in complete harmony with the will of God? I cannot even begin to imagine it. I sink even before I start. And I have heard enough confessions from high-ranking religious "stalwarts" to make me think that this must be a universal trait.

Given this background, which I believe is a correct reflection of our moral condition, His perfection seems so far removed from the reality of everyday life that it is difficult to accept it with confidence. It was much easier to view Him as a "plastic" saint: manufactured according to a computerized plan, artificially dressed and painted-up, without a flaw, and programmed never to fail—so utterly unlike me! But since many people and religious leaders called Him perfect, I have a choice. I can follow suit, in meaningless, parrot-like repetition, or dismiss it as a tall story. But the report came from those who actually lived with Him. They seemed to portray a real person, and if I choose to disbelieve them, what reason can I give for my stand?

And what if He was truly without taint? What if that life was actually lived to unblemished perfection? What then? How would I go about refuting the written reports of eyewitnesses, who obviously watched Him closely from day to day for months and years at a stretch? Facing His bitter, blood-thirsty critics, He once challenged them to point out a sin in Him—only to receive silence as the answer. How many such examples can we find, combing through society and history? Great, admirable lives have shrunk from claiming perfection. "How dare I claim to be a sage or a benevolent man?" asked Confucius, the founder of Confucianism. Not only did Jesus make the claim, but nobody seemed to have been able to disprove it.

We live on at least three levels. The first is the physical—the place of our actions. The second is the mental dimension of thoughts and plans—that which governs the actions. The third is deep—the world of motives and conscience. We could make a case for doing right, such as speaking appropriately with a smile or giving donations generously. When it comes to the second, it becomes more and more difficult to be completely correct and pure. By the time we reach our motives, we are undone. We must confess how self-centered we really are—how unlike Him. So distant are we from the goal that it seems more practical and convenient to make our own reference points and then rationalize our behavior. But rationalizations cannot wipe the conscience clean. We can temporarily fend off the peripheral issues, but an honest inquiry into our motives shows how powerless we are to do anything about our bent to selfishness and moral lapses. So to find someone who claimed to be otherwise, during an entire lifetime, is remarkable beyond words.

> **"Fifteen million minutes of life on this earth, in the midst of a wicked and corrupt generation—every thought, every deed, every purpose, every work, privately and publicly, from the time He opened His baby eyes until He expired on the cross, were all approved of God. Never once did our Lord have to confess sin for He had no sin"** (Wilbur Smith, quoted in NEDV, p. 311).

> **"He, and He alone carried the spotless purity of childhood untarnished through youth and manhood"** (Philip Schaff, quoted in NEDV, p. 310). **"Christ's self-conscious purity is astonishing"** (McDowell, NEDV, p. 307). **"He remains the highest model of religion within the reach of our thought..."** (David Strauss, quoted in NEDV, p. 312).

There was also the internal consistency in His claims that I could not dismiss (see p. 114).

> **"Sinless perfection and perfect sinlessness is what we would expect of God-incarnate, and this we find in Jesus Christ. The hypothesis and facts concur."** Bernard Ramm, *Protestant Christian Evidences* (Chicago, IL: Moody Press, 1957), p. 169.

He stands before us in His perfection—unique in every sense of the word!

3. Greatest Words

When public speeches are made, it is often a combination of position, fame, insight, wittiness, and oratorical skills that get our attention and grip the imagination. Such words/speeches appeal to our emotions and can even bring a sense of enjoyment similar to when we are entertained. However, every so often a person comes along whose background is ordinary, even lowly, and completely devoid of the usual trappings of greatness, but whose words are so unexpected and piercing that they catch us off guard and push our thoughts to paths and realms we had not envisioned before. The concepts and principles remain etched for a long time. Jesus seemed to belong to that category. Scholars and common folk alike have been captivated by His words, teachings, and methods of communication.

Since his background was carpentry by trade, and his family was probably too poor to afford the rabbinical schools of His day, it is all the more amazing.

> **"Without science and learning, He shed more light on things human and divine than all philosophers and scholars combined; without the eloquence of schools, He spoke such words of life as were never spoken before or since . . . without writing a single line, He set more pens in motion, and furnished themes for more sermons, orations, discussions, learned volumes, works of art, and songs of praise, than the whole army of great men of ancient and modern times"** (Philip Schaff, quoted in NEDV, p. 321).

> **"They are read more, quoted more, loved more, believed more and translated more because they are the greatest words ever spoken"** (Bernard Ramm, quoted in NEDV, p. 320).

On thinking further, it is in line with His claim of having come from a divine realm. He seemed to have an aura about Him, and even though His words were so simple and direct that ordinary peasants were able to catch the meaning and significance, they had a depth and a ring of truth to them that the craftiest Pharisee could not overturn or deny. They belonged to a different category.

> **"After reading the doctrines of Plato, Socrates or Aristotle, we feel the specific difference between their words and Christ's is the difference between an inquiry and a revelation"** (Joseph Parker, quoted in NEDV, p. 319).

But no matter how impressive and gripping, words tend to lose their force as time goes by. They become less and less a part of our conscious thinking, and we tend to move on to more modern and updated concepts and ideas. This is just the way things happen. No author would feel badly that later generations did not place the same emphasis on his writings as his own had done, and no author ever claimed that his words were there to stay. But this Man obviously had something else in mind. Time was not going to be a factor.

> **"Heaven and earth shall pass away, but My words shall not pass away"** (Matthew 24:35).

Really? Wow!

> **"Never did the Speaker seem to stand more utterly alone than when He uttered this majestic utterance. Never did it seem more *improbable* that it should be fulfilled. But as we look across the centuries we see how it has been realized . . . they have never 'passed away.' What human teacher ever dared to claim an eternity for His words?"** (G. F. Maclean, quoted in NEDV, p. 320, italics supplied).

Utterly alone, in a class by Himself, far removed from what the rest of history attempted to teach, He spoke words that brought a message so unique that it changed the course of human thought decisively and permanently.

> **"Never man spoke like this Man"**! (John 7:46).

4. Miracles

Whether we are openly accepting or grudgingly reticent about it, the historicity of the Man Jesus has been acknowledged and acceded to by a wide spectrum of scholars. The record of His life, sketchy by today's standards, is contained in literature that has to be classified as historical and not mythological or legendary (see chapter 3, Section One). Yes, we do find what appear to be parallel descriptions in mythological accounts. The blind, the deaf, the mute, and the paralyzed are healed instantly; a fearful storm is ordered to stop; food is multiplied limitlessly; demons are exorcised with a single command; and even the dead are raised to life. These examples would naturally tempt us to think that the miracles in the Gospels, too, belong to the same category, but at least five significant differences distinguish them from myths:

They were not embellished

Bizarre, fanciful embellishments, in great numbers, permeate myths. As C. S. Lewis stated, one can detect the "flavor" of a myth after reading a number of them. Described with much fanfare, they are made quite the center of the narrative, with the intent of calling attention to them. Such is not the case in the Gospels. Instead of containing added exaggerations, the Gospels evidence a distinct effort to downplay them. Not described in glowing, admiring terms, they are simply called the "works" of Jesus. In instances of healing, Jesus is reported to have earnestly instructed the person not to speak publicly about it. This stands in clear contrast to mythological accounts.

The miracles had a very specific purpose

His focus was not on the catchy, flashy stuff that would naturally have caused excitement but rather, on the deep need of the person(s) before Him. Of course, the miracles were exciting to the public, and word spread like wildfire about them, but that is not the reason they were performed. A good look at the spectrum (which included physical healing, command over nature, and even raising from the dead), and the circumstances in which they were done, show that they were performed to bring hope, healing, and courage to the person and then to give God the credit and praise. He did not do them for self-promotion, with a yearning to display His abilities and powers publicly. His motives were pure and grounded in love. He performed His miracles with only the recipient's good in mind.

The miracles were done openly

Witnessed by the public, the miracles were therefore open to testing and evaluation, even by enemies. The ones who reported them were actually present in person and could rightfully say, "I saw it for myself." And they were written down in the same generation as these events, leaving little room for gradual embellishments to creep in and change the story from the actual to the stretched out and amplified. No other ancient writing has such a credible record.

The miracles have extra-biblical testimony

The Quran, in chapter 5, verse 10, speaks of Jesus healing the blind and the lepers and also raising the dead.

The Jewish writings attest to the unusual—**"Around AD 95 Rabbi Eliezer ben Hyrcanus of Lydda speaks of Jesus' magic arts"** (Ethelbert Stauffer, quoted in NEDV, p. 314).

Julian, the Roman Emperor from A.D. 361 to 363, made references to **"heal the lame and blind people and exorcise demoniacs in the villages of Bethsaida and Bethany"** (Philip Schaff, quoted in NEDV, p. 315).

Such testimonies, from diverse sources other than the writing/religion itself, should impress us with the probable truthfulness of those far-away events.

The miracles were critical to faith.

Because they were real-life events and not mythical inventions, the role they played in the faith of the community was crucial.

> **"Miracles are believed in non-Christian religions because the religion is already believed, but in the Biblical religion, miracles are part of the means of establishing the true religion. This distinction is of immense importance. Israel was brought into existence by a series of miracles. . . . It was the miracle authenticating the religion at every point"** (Bernard Ramm, quoted in NEDV, p. 315).

> **"It [Christianity] is precisely the story of a great Miracle. A naturalistic Christianity leaves out all that is specifically Christian"** (C. S. Lewis, quoted in NEDV, p. 315).

Unusual events that seem far-fetched and drive us toward disbelief cannot form the base of a claim, unless they can be reasonably established as having actually occurred. The only way to gauge this in something written thousands of years ago is to inspect the writing itself. If it turns out to be an eyewitness account of a deed performed in public, with enemies not making any attempt to discredit the account, there is every reason to accept it as trustworthy. Even in the most unbelievable story, of raising someone from the dead (Lazarus) who had been in the tomb for four days, there is no record of His enemies trying to controvert the report. They obviously could not deny the miracle. The record states that many believed in Him because of the unusual powers He displayed.

Miracles are recorded in other writings, too, but Jesus still stands apart, because, unlike the other performers, such as Muhammad (the writing of the Quran is claimed to be a miracle) or Moses (the parting the Red Sea), He belonged to the Source of the miracle—the Godhead. All the others confessed that the power for their miracles came, not from themselves, but externally, from God. Jesus claimed to *be* that God Himself!

Multiple miracles, authenticated by friends as well as enemies and performed by One who claimed to have intimate and personal access to the Power required to accomplish them, is a feature unmatched in history.

5. Addressed Deep Needs

The biography of this Man is very brief, as compared to today's literature. But such was the style and intent of writing in those days. John, one of the biographers, confessed that the story was actually so full of numerous other events and episodes that **"even the whole world itself could not contain the books that would be written"** (John 21:25), yet he wrote down only a few of them. I suppose he felt he had done enough to show the pattern—the flavor and the personification—of the real intent of God regarding humans. That intent was to help us, not in just a passing and superficial way, but by going to the depths of our lives and addressing the fears, the guilt, the apprehensions, and the helplessness that is the common lot of humanity and that often come in unrelenting waves of despair and hopelessness. No matter what the circumstance, He probed the depths, so He could bring help, healing, and hope to those areas of life that really mattered. Contemplate the deep understanding and tender consideration of our condition in His invitation, **"Come unto Me all who are weary and heavy laden . . . and I will give you rest"** (Matthew 11:28). **"If anyone thirsts, let him come to Me and drink"** (John 7:37).

What can be more basic than being burdened in life and feeling thirsty? What can run deeper in emotions than when we are unable to fulfill those basic needs? Every teaching, every parable, and every miracle touched some fundamental, distressing need of the person(s) before Him. He was not interested in creating excitement. He was on a mission to find the most despairing and provide an answer to the cries that came from the depths of that heart. **"He addressed the naked heart of man and touched the quick of the conscience"** (Philip Schaff, quoted in NEDV, p. 325).

We are prone to try our own methods to address our needs. We go looking for what I describe as the "Five Ps"—Possession, Position, Popularity, Power, and Pleasure (that ultimately cause the sixth P—Pain). And after having had our fill of these, the honest evaluation is that they are, in the long run, as tasty and nourishing as sawdust! We did not even know what we were looking for. But He seemed to have known all along and addressed the real nature of that thirst and hunger.

"My peace I give to you; not as the world gives. . . . Let not your heart be troubled, neither let it be afraid" (John 14:27). The problems of this world are more than adequately met and answered by a peace (the seventh P—Peace!) **"which surpasses all understanding"** (Philippians 4:7). This peace need not still the storm but can hold the heart above it. After the cravings and heated desires are chased after and clawed for—some attained and others left unfulfilled—there comes a deep yearning for contentment and peace. After shedding all the layers and façades that we develop and strap on, when we come to the naked core, there He is, ready to understand and bring help, hope, and healing.

"I became a Christian because I found in myself a need which could be satisfied only by Jesus Christ" (R. L. Mixter, quoted in NEDV, p. 326).

To those who have found Him thus, He will always remain the unique problem-solver; some go so far as to call Him "The Fairest of Ten Thousand," "The Rose of Sharon," and "The One Altogether Lovely." Because what He proffers leads to restfulness, He becomes refreshing and welcome to the pressed and burdened soul.

Who else can seek so earnestly, approach so caringly, delve so deeply, and apply the balm so soothingly! "Unique" must be His name!

6. Lasting Influence

Walking through a cemetery, one can pass hundreds of plaques, tombstones, headstones, and markers without recognizing any of the names. Some sites have elaborate structures with ornate trimmings, carvings, and gold and precious gems that adorn the edifice. One of the most famous is the Taj Mahal in Agra, India (one of the Seven Wonders of the World) built by the Moghul Emperor Shah Jahan for the love of his life—his spouse, Mumtaz Mahal. Yet today, only those familiar with that history know the names behind the monument. Westminster Abbey, another famous spot in London, England, has perpetuated the names of the "greats" of the times in which they lived. The effort and resources spent in erecting such impressive buildings were meant to keep the memory of these alive. Yet how many of those names are familiar to the billions on earth today? Very few, I reckon. They all seem to become hazier, as time goes by.

Turning our gaze in the direction of Jesus, we find a difference. From the dimly lit pages of those faraway times comes the story of One who appears to continue to glow. Time, the inexorable destroyer of recorded exploits and memories, has failed to rob Him of luster.

"The sages and heroes of history are receding from us, and history contracts the record of their deeds into a narrower and narrower page. But time has no power over the name and deeds and words of Jesus Christ" (William E. Channing, quoted in NEDV, p. 323).

Why did He not pass off the scene as did the others?

"Superficial minds see a resemblance between Christ and the founders of empires and the gods of other religions. That resemblance does not exist. There is between Christianity and whatever

> **other religions the distance of infinity"** (Napoleon Bonaparte, quoted in NEDV, p. 161).

For a common peasant's name even to have survived a few generations would have been remarkable. For people to be familiar with it today, 2,000 years later, is awe-inspiring. But even more striking is that it has not only managed to survive but has dominated the landscape, touching nearly all major aspects of life on earth.

> **"It may be truly said that the simple record of three short years of active life has done more to regenerate and soften mankind than all the disquisitions of philosophies and all the exhortations of moralists"** (William Lecky, quoted in NEDV, p. 322).

Perhaps it is not evident in the fast and furious pace of our lives, but in our more contemplative moments, when reflecting on the effects of that life, it can be seen to permeate the depths of society the world over. Yes, it must be conceded that Christianity has received severe negative publicity in different ages, because of those who bear the name yet pervert the message. But once we go beyond this admission, the scene changes. In His name, the hungry are fed, the ignorant are schooled, the downtrodden uplifted, and the oppressed released. To sit on the sidelines casting aspersions on the motives of those who bring about the change is one thing; it is quite another to be the recipient and have heavy shackles removed and hope revived, where once only despair reigned. If the motives are to be questioned, let us not, in doing that, begrudge the hungry some bread, the ravaged a touch of healing, and the wretched a glimmer of hope. D. James Kennedy and Jerry Newcombe described the effects of Jesus and Christianity on history, in a book titled *What If Jesus Had Never Been Born?* (Nashville, TN: Thomas Nelson, 1994).

Here is a partial list of what they cite:

- Hospitals, which essentially began during the Middle Ages.
- Universities, which also began during the Middle Ages. Some of the world's greatest universities were started by Christians.
- Civil liberties and the abolition of slavery, both in antiquity and in modern times.
- Benevolence and charity—the Good Samaritan ethic.
- Higher standards of justice.

- The high regard for human life.
- The civilization of many barbarian and primitive cultures.
- The codifying and setting to writing of many of the world's languages.
- The inspiration for the greatest works of art.

None of these is small or minor. To have been the springboard of even one would have been to attach lasting fame to His name. To have been the origination and catalyst of a *paradigm shift* in human thinking and endeavors is to be acknowledged as the rudder that directed the course of history.

"Jesus Christ as the God-man is the greatest personality that ever lived and therefore His personal impact is the greatest of any man that ever lived" (Bernard Ramm, quoted in NEDV, p. 318).

"Jesus Christ is the outstanding personality of all time . . . He became the Light of the World. Why shouldn't I, a Jew, be proud of that" (Sholem Ash, quoted in NEDV, p. 319).

When H. G. Wells was asked which person had left the most permanent impression on history, he replied:

"By this test (judging a person's greatness by historical standards) Jesus stands first" (quoted in NEDV, p. 318).

"As the centuries pass the evidence is accumulating that, measured by His effect on history, Jesus is the most influential life ever lived on this planet" (Kenneth Scott Latourette, quoted in NEDV, p. 321).

How did He influence life on Planet Earth in such a decisive manner, when He had nothing that is usually attached to greatness? He was born in a dirty stable in morally questionable circumstances; grew up in a village notorious for bad behavior; lived in poverty as a carpenter and then turned into an itinerant village preacher by choice; was rejected by His community and nation; and finally, died as a criminal under the curse of God. That ending portrayed a complete disaster—the exact opposite of what we would normally construe as the end to a noble, influential life. Yet influence the human race He did—and in unequalled magnitude! The evidence is there for all to see.

7. Conquered Death

The principle of life is a total mystery to humans. What is it that makes anything alive? That entity, quality, or power has never been isolated or defined. It exists in various forms but has never been identified apart from matter. Therefore, the mystery of life has remained unraveled. For this reason, death, too, has not been characterized in universally acceptable terms. To some, it is the cessation of life; to others, it is equated with sleep; to yet others, it is a transition to another form of life and even another form of existence itself! Whatever the definition/concept, and however sincere the attempt to teach it as welcome and acceptable, it is the most feared and unwelcome of all events. The eulogies and flowers, feasts and ceremonies, have not been able to alleviate the piercing pain and agony or to fill the aching void and loneliness that is associated with the loss.

Who can deny or downplay those emotions that plunge the soul to uncontrollable depths of despair? Who can claim to stay that icy hand and bring it into subjection rather than be subject to it? Here the monarch is made to bow low, the emperor is subjugated like a hapless commoner, and the mightiest general forced to surrender. Who can stand? "No one!" had been the mournful, desolate cry of history, till a lowly peasant, this Galilean carpenter, stepped onto the scene and staked His claim as the Teacher of ultimate Truth and the undisputed handler of death and destiny.

> **"Here is a teacher of religion and He calmly professes to stake His entire claims upon His ability, after being done to death, to rise again from the grave. We may safely assume that there never was, before or since, such a proposal made"** (R. M'Cheyne Edgar, quoted in NEDV, p. 207).

> **"When He said that He himself would rise again from the dead . . . He said something that only a fool would dare say. . . . No founder of any religion known to men ever dared say a thing like that!"** (Wilbur Smith, quoted in NEDV, p. 208).

Who could He really be? What kind of authority did He wield?

> **"When asked for a sign, He pointed to this sign as His simple and sufficient credential"** (B. B. Warfield, quoted in NEDV, p. 208). **"He who was ready to stake everything on His ability to come back from the tomb stands before us as the most original of all teachers"** (R. M'Cheyne Edgar, quoted in NEDV, p. 207).

The story claims that things came to a head and reached a breathtaking finale on a Sunday morning, when He who was dead and buried rose to life, leaving behind only grave clothes in an otherwise empty tomb.

"The bones of Abraham and Muhammad and Buddha and Confucius and Lao-Tzu and Zoroaster are still here on earth. Jesus' tomb is empty" (P. Kreeft and R. K. Tacelli, quoted in NEDV, p. 208).

The biggest and most pertinent question is whether or not it really happened. While there is no way to prove it to an absolute degree, the opposite is also valid—there is no way to disprove it.

"The scientist who is true to the philosophy of science can doubt the bodily resurrection of Jesus Christ, but he cannot deny it" (A. C. Ivy, quoted in NEDV, p. 219).

If both claims cannot be proved, we are left with the present historical evidence that may be scrutinized and weighed out (see chapter 12 of Section One).

"On that greatest point we are not merely asked to have faith. In its favor as living truth, there exists such overwhelming evidence, positive and negative, factual and circumstantial, that no intelligent jury in the world could fail to bring in a verdict that the resurrection story is true" (Lord Darling, Chief Justice of England, quoted in NEDV, p. 219).

Imagine the chief justice of a nation using the words *overwhelming evidence* in his ruling in a court of law, before sounding the gavel! The strength of such an expression should make us take note. And if we do, then looking over the landscape of history, only One appears who made the claim, handled death, and tamed it.

"He alone of all men who ever lived, conquered death itself. . . . He said, 'Because I live, ye shall live also.' John 14:19" (Henry Morris, quoted in NEDV, p. 327).

"Nineteen centuries have come and gone, and today He is the centerpiece of the human race and the leader of the column of progress. I am far within the mark when I say that all the armies that ever marched, all the navies ever built, all the parliaments that ever sat and all the kings that ever reigned, put together, have not affected the life of man upon this earth as powerfully as has that one solitary life" (Anonymous, quoted in NEDV, p. 324).

"Jesus is not one of the world's greats—He is THE ONLY!"

16

The Book

This book, the Bible, consists of sixty-six sections which were written as separate "books." Thirty-nine were written before the time of Jesus the Christ and are called the Old Testament, or The Law and Prophets. Twenty-seven came after the life of Jesus and are collectively known as the New Testament. The Old Testament is Judaic, while the New Testament is Christian. However, Christians consider the Old Testament to be valid because it was sent down from the same "Source" that inspired the New. Based on that, their scripture should really be called Judeo-Christian.

Do these Judeo-Christian scriptures possess qualities so extraordinary that they can elicit admiration, amazement, and even awe? Here are seven features I found that deserve to be considered:

1. The way it was written
2. The amazing harmony
3. Widespread influence
4. Textual preservation
5. Survival although banished
6. Sale and circulation
7. Extensive translation

Let us examine each of these:

1. The Way It Was Written

a. The Extended Period of Writing

The first author most probably was Moses, whose initial work was supposed to be the book of Job. This was about 1300 B.C. to 1400 B.C. Following came a lengthy string of writers reaching to the close of the first century A.D., when John wrote the last book which was included in this set. That would be a period of at least 1,400 years spanning generations, historical ages, and multiple cultures—a unique feature.

b. Diverse Background of Authors

More than forty authors wrote, from vastly differing ranks and stations in life.

- Moses was educated in the most prestigious Egyptian centers of learning of his day. He was a statesman, judge, political leader, teacher, and a top-rated organizer.

- Joshua was a military general trained by apprenticeship.
- Samuel was a priest, prophet, and judge.
- David was a shepherd, poet, musician, king, and warrior.
- Daniel was a ranking diplomat, holding one of the highest governmental positions in two successive world empires—the Babylonian and the Medo-Persian.
- Amos was a herdsman.
- Luke was a physician, traveler, and recently rated by none other than Sir William Ramsay (one of the greatest archaeologists ever), as a historian par excellence.
- Peter was a fisherman.
- Matthew was a tax collector.
- Paul was a Jewish rabbi.
- Mark was a personal attendant and secretary.

This vast spectrum, from nobility to the lowly, from the learned to the simple, defies any attempt at a coherent classification.

c. Differing Circumstances

- Moses wrote mainly while traveling as the head of a huge nomadic group who had been slaves for generations. He was their leader, judge, and military general.
- A scribe recorded some of Jeremiah's messages, spoken when he was thrown into a dungeon for allegedly not being patriotic enough.
- Daniel wrote while at his home, as well as in the palace of a world emperor.
- David's writings were spread over a lifetime—sometimes as an outlaw hiding in a cave and later, as a king.
- Paul wrote while traveling as a free man and also when locked up in prison as a convict.
- Luke kept a diary for years while on extensive travels over land and sea.

- John wrote in lonely exile on a deserted island.

d. Fluctuating Times and Moods

- Moses wrote while an undisputed but often exhausted and exasperated head of a nation.
- David's expressions were of both abject fear for his life, when hunted as a fugitive, and the declarations of a confident king.
- Solomon wrote when young and giddy with abundance and prosperity, as well as when age and sober reflection seemed to reduce everything in life to ashes.
- Daniel was strong and poised in his declarations, yet at other times, completely perplexed as to what he himself had written down.
- Jeremiah wrote in deep grief and bitterness of spirit.
- Isaiah expressed solid conviction and certainty.
- Luke maintained exactness and detail, as an honest, credible historian.
- Paul wrote with the sternness, as well as the tenderness of a father.

e. Different Styles of Expression

- Story-telling—Genesis and Esther
- Historical documentation—Chronicles and Kings
- Poetry and song—Psalms
- Romance—Song of Solomon
- Didactic treatise—Proverbs
- Personal correspondence—Paul's Epistles
- Memoirs—Acts
- Biography—Gospel of Luke
- Autobiography—Ezekiel
- Code of Law—Leviticus and Deuteronomy

- Prophetic Declarations—Isaiah, Jeremiah, Daniel, Revelation
- Parables and Allegories—The Gospels

f. Three Continents

- Asia
- Europe
- Africa

g. Three Languages

- Hebrew
- Greek
- Aramaic

2. Amazing Harmony

If one common theme went through the last section, it was that everything was different: different time periods, different authors, different circumstances, different moods, different styles, different continents, and different languages.

Yet it is *one* book, with a *single* story—that of the history of the world; and *one* theme—the subterranean and often hidden conflict between "good and evil."

More than that, it has *one* lead character throughout—from Genesis to Revelation—Jesus of Nazareth, the Christ.

For a perspective, let's imagine randomly picking ten individuals from different countries, different cultures, and from a period spread over three to four centuries, and inviting them to write whatever they felt compelled to write, from deep within. The ten would include a servant, a president, a teacher, a shepherd, a businessman, an astronaut, a farmer, a military general, a university professor, and a priest. What would be the chances of their writing on the same broad subjects, such as health, history, business, or psychology? Would they endorse one another's views? If they chose history, would they all have the same story, with the same lead character?

No work of fiction can maintain a single story, while being written in the manner the Bible was written—by scores of writers, over such an extended period—unless it was supervised and directed from beginning to end. Therefore, it is reasonable to think that it is a *real* story, with a theme and plot that really existed and was played out in *real* life, and that it had a single hero who was *real!*

But that is exactly what is claimed. The attesting cross-references between authors of the Old Testament, between authors of the New Testament, and between authors of the Old and New Testament (described in the chapter "Top Feature" in my previous section), clearly suggest that there was a single "Source" called "The Lord" who supervised the writing throughout the 1,400 years.

To propose a natural, everyday explanation to such unusual features is extremely difficult.

3. Widespread and Persisting Influence

> **"Since the dawn of civilization no book has inspired as much creative endeavor among writers"** (Gabriel Sivan, quoted in NEDV, p. 14).

> **"Its impact has no equal whether on the social and ethical plane or on that of literary creation"** (Elie Wiesel, quoted in NEDV, p. 14).

> **"Western literature has been more influenced by the Bible than any other book"** (Northrop Frye, quoted in NEDV, p. 15).

> **"No other book in all human history has in turn inspired the writing of so many books as the Bible"** (Bernard Ramm, quoted in NEDV, p. 15).

> **"Civilization has been influenced more by the Judeo-Christain Scriptures than by any other book or series of books in the world"** (Norman Geisler, quoted in NEDV, p. 15).

Not alone unique is the widespread nature of the influence of the Bible—although that in itself is impressive—but also the fact that it has persisted for thousands of years. Christian believers are not the only ones impressed. The literary and educational world, the entertainment and music world, the world of social and humanitarian projects, have all turned, time and again, to this book for themes to uplift and bring meaning and purpose to our lives on Planet Earth.

We are prone to treat it as mundane, because it is such a commonly available book. We seem to be attracted by only the rare. But the very fact that it is commonly available is a rare credit, because it is such an ancient book, yet surprisingly, is still available today. Widely accepted, it is still effective, and it still changes lives for the better and has still retained its appeal—probably more so now than ever before.

4. Meticulously Preserved

"Jews preserved it as no other manuscript has ever been preserved.

... They kept tabs on every letter, syllable, word and paragraph. Who ever counted the words of Plato, Aristotle? Cicero or Seneca?" (Bernard Ramm, quoted in NEDV, p. 15).

" ... For 2300 to 3900 years the text of proper names has been transmitted with the most minute accuracy ... a phenomenon unequaled in the history of literature" (Robert Dick Wilson, quoted in NEDV, p. 70).

" ... It may be safely said that no other work of antiquity has been so accurately transmitted" (William Green, quoted in NEDV, p. 71).

The Bible was an ancient writing. No printing presses or other forms of technology existed, to ensure ease of production and accuracy. But it was copied with the most meticulous care. No other text has been backed by generations of professional copiers trained for just that one particular task—striving to make each copy as perfect a reproduction of the original as possible. The standards they set for themselves were unusually rigid, exacting, and high, and they maintained them.

Let's compare this with a relatively modern text. Shakespeare's works came onto the scene after printing presses were in use for centuries. What is the credibility of that text today?

"In every one of the twenty-seven plays of Shakespeare there are dozens of disputed portions that are large and that can change the meaning of the text." John Lea, *The Greatest Book in the World* (Philadelphia, n.p., 1929), p. 15.

Such comparisons serve to highlight the astonishing accuracy of the text of the Judeo-Christian scripture, which has been amazingly and accurately preserved.

5. Saga of Survival

Many books have been rejected and discarded by a group or community, at some time or another. But later, they were forgotten or ignored. Other books earned such ire as to be publicly burned and are now extinct. But the Bible's existence is like the swings of a pendulum. During some periods, it has been accepted with deep devotion by millions. At other times, it has elicited an unusual degree of sustained hatred and rage, lasting generations. No other book in history has been so repeatedly banished and endured so many attempts to destroy it completely. No other book sprang back stronger and became more widespread than before. What reasons were held, to destroy it?

I believe there could be two factors:

The first: The Bible's radical claims, which have been quite disconcerting to many. For example, it claims that Jesus is not a mere man but God. So it requires complete submission to the principles He taught, leaving no room for indifference to, or evasion of, the question. While this could be evidence for "rampant megalomania" (C. S. Lewis), the evidences it furnishes to sustain the claim of Jesus' divinity does not allow an easy, quick dismissal. So the irritation remains.

The discomfort worsens as it confronts and mercilessly rebukes the inherent clamor for position, power, and self-importance in us. It probes deep, to the level of the heart, as if restless till it gets a response.

> **"Jesus Christ makes a demand which is beyond all others difficult to satisfy.... He asks for the human heart; He will have it entirely to Himself; He demands it unconditionally, and forthwith His demand is granted.... This phenomenon is unaccountable, it is altogether beyond the scope of man's creative powers."** (Napoleon Bonaparte, quoted in NEDV, pp. 322, 323).

The second: The Bible's radical effects on human lives. Loyalty shifts away from human authority, and that makes it unsettling to the powers that be. The followers now have a devotion to the Book and the Man that no power on earth can destroy. Everyone else becomes secondary, and no threat, however severe, can deter them. Unwittingly, they portray a picture of defiance and near invincibility. This probably is what unnerves even kings and emperors, who, unable to control or handle it, resort to persecution and a determined plan to crush the source of the problem—the Book!

No wonder.

> **"No other book has been so chopped, knived, sifted, scrutinized and vilified ... upon every chapter, line and tenet"** (Bernard Ramm, quoted in NEDV, p. 11).

> **"Emperors and popes, kings and priests, princes and rulers have all tried their hands at it; they die and the book still lives"** (H. L. Hastings, quoted in NEDV, p. 11).

A classic example of this is the case of Voltaire, the French atheist who died in 1778. He had predicted that Christianity would be wiped out within a hundred years. Not only was this proved false, but

"Only fifty years after his death, the Geneva Bible Society used Voltaire's press and house to produce stacks of Bibles!" (Geisler and Nix, quoted in NEDV, p. 10).

Why the swing of the pendulum between hatred and acceptance; between destruction and survival? Because the reason for wanting the Book swept out of existence (its radical claims and its radical effects on people's lives) forms the basis for its survival! If you hate an object because it will not catch fire and choose to destroy it by burning, it will survive, no matter how much it is hated or how hot the furnace. The only way to burn it is to remove that quality which is protecting it from the fire. If that quality cannot be removed, then it will survive. To remove the radical claims from the Book or disregard the changes in people's lives is impossible. Therefore, it must survive.

One look around the world will testify that it has not only survived, it has thrived and flourished. Read on.

6. Phenomenal Circulation

"Oh, to reach the best seller status!" sighs every hopeful, budding author, because, on average, a new book sells only about a thousand copies. So when best seller status is reached, it is time for celebration. If the number climbs to the million mark, fame is attached to the author's name, and people look out for his or her next work. If the number rises to the tens of millions, it becomes a rare achievement. Only a small fraction of writers ever reach that stage.

What makes the numbers go up? Multiple factors are at work, but I think two are crucial. The content has to be relevant in some way, and it must produce effects that grip the reader. Only then will word about the book spread. Every "successful" book has had that critical word-of-mouth publicity, which gave it the push to take it that far.

The first types of "best sellers" that come to mind are novels and other fictional works, in which descriptions of every sort can be woven in, at will, to lure and hold the reader. What kind of circulation, then, would we expect for the translation of ancient manuscripts written thousands of years ago? I would expect the number to be a few thousands—mainly from educational institutions and the experts in that particular field of study. However, the numbers would go up if the material were found to be relevant and applicable to the common people today. It would cause wonder that something so old could still have validity in modern times. If, in addition, the writing revealed the answer to a universal concern, such as, for example, the secrets of youth and longevity, and if there were sufficient testimonials to its credibility, the masses would go running for it. I can see the numbers rise to the tens of millions.

The Bible is a series of books, the earliest of which was written about 3,500 years ago and the latest about 2,000 years past. They belong to the category of the very ancient.

Yet their distribution holds an all-time record, beating the top ten *New York Times* best sellers combined, and by a margin that's almost embarrassing. Bibles sold number not just in the tens of millions. Here's a report of one year. The **"United Bible Societies' 1998 Scripture Distribution Report ... the total distribution of copies of the Bible or portions thereof in 1998 reaches a staggering 585 million ..."** (NEDV, p. 8).

Does the number say anything about its relevance and grip on people today? Does it not point to a massive wave of word-of-mouth publicity? To pass off such a "staggering" number and treat it as mundane and ordinary would not be fair. No other book or series of books can come even within sight for a comparison!

7. Unmatched Translation

According to a United Nations report, there are about 6,000 languages in the world today. The first 1,000 would probably cover 90 percent to 95 percent of the world's population, the rest being scattered among smaller and smaller groups, with the final few hundred covering only a minute fraction of the whole.

Writers produce their works in the language with which they are most comfortable and consider it an honor when there is a request to translate it into another language.

When translated into even two or three languages, it is usually an indication that the book has potential for widespread appeal, and is taken as a compliment. In fact, the more the requests, the greater the acknowledgment of its worth. When a book has been translated into ten languages, it can be considered a milestone. Osho's books on meditation and mysticism have been translated into over forty languages. Impressive! (Incidentally, he set up his meditation center in Koregaon Park in the city of Pune, India, where I grew up and spent my schooling years.) Another author, Ellen G. White, the most-prolific female nonfiction writer in history and the most-translated American nonfiction writer ever, has the record of being translated into over a hundred languages. Very impressive! And these are relatively modern works.

When it comes to the Bible, it has no equal.

It holds the distinction of being the first major book ever to be translated. The Hebrew Old Testament was translated into Greek more than two centuries before Christ. Seventy scholars helped complete the project, and that translation has been called the Septuagint. For those times and circumstances, it was a massive effort.

Since then, there has been a stream of translations, the pace of which has increased in the last few generations. Today, there seems to be an urgency in trying to get it translated into as many languages as possible.

> **"[The] Wycliffe Bible Translators alone has over six thousand people working with more than 850 different languages in fifty countries.... Of these, 468 languages are being translated for the first time"** (NEDV, p. 9).

How can any other writing even come close!

But that is not all.

> **"According to Ted Bergman at the Summer Institute of Linguistics, at this rate the Bible should be available to almost all language groups between 2007 and 2022. This means that we are less than a generation away from witnessing the world's first universally translated text!"** (NEDV, p. 9.)

Imagine one book garnering such multiple, top-ranking accolades:

- Historically—the first book translated
- Presently—the most translated work
- Tomorrow—the first, and probably the only, universally translated piece of literature

And this is not some flashy science fiction or earthy suspense thriller. Rather, it comprises copies of an ancient manuscript written from between 2,000 and 3,500 years ago. What might the contents be, for so many to be so interested in spending so much effort in undertaking so monumental a task?

These seven features together point to a caliber of literature that nothing on the horizon can equal. The Bible has set a standard all its own and now sits on a pedestal, destined to remain unsurpassed—unquestionably one of a kind! Could it be the voice from another world?

17

Gospel

The word *gospel* comes from the Greek "euangelion," which means "good news." Before Christ, it was known for centuries but was not in common use. The word was heard infrequently and in rather specific circumstances. "Euangelion" did not refer to news that was just good—but also to the circumstances in which it arrived. The background was one of hopelessness, devastation, and utter ruin, against which the news came, bringing with it a complete reversal of mood, spirit, and hope. The terrifying nature of the crisis ahead was what accentuated the thrill of the news and gave it that exquisite touch called *euangelion.* For example, the army had gone out to battle against a cruel, ruthless enemy known to be vastly superior in number, armor, and equipment, and there appeared very little chance of success. The only realistic outcome was going to be defeat, plunder, torture, rape, slavery, and death. But then the watchman sees in the distance a messenger from the battlefield, and he is signaling victory. What welcome news! "Euangelion!" he shouts out, and that word is echoed throughout the land, transforming despair and impending doom to the heights of triumphant celebration.

The city of Alexandria, in northern Africa, had very few agricultural resources in ancient times and depended entirely on grain brought by ships from Phoenicia—present-day Lebanon. As the supplies in the barrels dwindled and the specter of famine and starvation reared its ugly head, all eyes turned toward the sea. When the last few measures of grain were being rationed out, some would climb to the highest points in the landscape to scan the watery horizon. Then, suddenly, there would ring out the cry "Euangelion!" The masts of the ships had been sighted. Starvation and death would hound them no more that year. Helplessness and apprehension gave way to song and dance. What rejoicing!

The New Testament writers chose this word as the synopsis of their message about Jesus. Inherent in the word was a message that, while the initial condition was one of dark despair and hopeless ruin, this Man had come, and now everything was being transformed to hope, joy, and abundance. Good news!

The Initial Condition

How welcome can we suppose bottled drinking water would be to a bunch of bachelors having a swinging party, with the best alcoholic beverages freely available at the bar? Would it be attractive even if the water were from some exotic glacier and bottled just for that party?

Take that same water and offer it to the same people, but this time in a different setting. They have been on a trek across the desert, lost their way, and now are hot, exhausted, and thirsty. With parched lips and dried tongues sticking to the roofs of their mouths, they can hardly walk another step. What would the sight of cool, clear, spring water do to them now? Would they go for the bottles or wave them off in disdain, as they would have done at the party?

Cool drinking water is good news to the thirsty though not to the drunk swaggering about in a bar. Food is welcome to the hungry but not to the one who has just binged to the point of nausea. The story of Jesus is "gospel" to those who recognize and feel their condition. To those who "labor and are heavy laden" (and who isn't!), it is attractive, because what is offered is "rest for your souls" (Matthew 11:28-30) It is "euangelion," because the condition couldn't have been worse and the news couldn't have been better!

What is that condition?

First, it is universal. Second, it is utterly hopeless.

Universal

The Book describes it in unequivocal terms:

> **"There is none righteous, no, not one; There is none who understands; There is none who seeks after God. They have *all* gone out of the way; ... There is none who does good, no, not one"** (Romans 3:10-12, quoted from Psalm 14:1-3). **"...There is no difference; for *all* have sinned and come short of the glory of God"** (Romans 3:22, 23).

A difference may be noted between the outward behavior of the pious monk in a monastery and that of the foul-mouthed, incurable drunk sprawled out on the roadside, or between the Bible-thumping preacher and the kingpin of a drug cartel, but the insides of each need to be drastically changed. *All* are alike—unrighteous in their hearts and nature.

Is an explanation available for this all-pervading picture? Yes, and it takes us to the dawn of history. Adam and Eve were the first humans—the progenitors of the human race. They were created in a state of innocence, and at that point, had no experience of going against God, which is sin. They did not have a bent or inclination toward it. Their hearts and minds were tuned to love as God loved. But they were also free moral agents and had the freedom to choose what they thought best regarding any issue confronting them.

Their state of innocence was dependent on making the right choices. One wrong choice would allow a principle other than love to slip in, take charge, and mitigate innocence. After that, there would be a bent and propensity to disobey God that would permeate the whole of life, leaving only the power of choice to go back to God but impairing the moral strength to deny that bent and inclination.

The first pair made a deliberate, wrong choice. Their nature twisted inward toward self-seeking rather than love. This warped trait has been passed on, in the genes, as it were, to every generation. The fabric of the race had been stained through and through, allowing no one to escape the deadly taint. Thus, **"there is none righteous, no, not one."**

Hopeless

The clearer the true picture of our condition, the chillier and more disheartening it gets. When we view A) the essence of the change, and B) the conditions for returning to innocence (paradise), all that remains is abject despair.

A. The Change.

It occurred in two aspects: 1) change in nature, and 2) change in leadership.

1. Change in Nature. This was three-fold.

a. Change in Direction: The goal now became to satisfy self, no matter the cost to anyone else. This was a change in principle and not primarily in behavior. Human nature was now self-centered. All behavior was going to be based on selfishness. The Bible uses the word *iniquity,* the root meaning of which is to be bent, twisted, deformed, and deficient. **"I was brought forth [born] in iniquity"** (Psalm 51:5).

b. Change in Ability: Because of iniquity (being bent and twisted), humans could no longer reach the standard. The best were still not up to the mark. The Bible uses the word *sin* to describe this. **"...** ***All*** **have sinned and** ***fall short*** **of the glory of God"** (Romans 3:23). Even after we have done all we know, we are still **"unprofitable servants"** (Luke 17:10).

c. Change in Will: Not only was there a deficiency in the attempt to do the right thing, there was a willful choice to do what was known to be wrong—and this was called transgression. **"You all have transgressed against Me"** (Jeremiah 2:29). This violation was done defiantly and was therefore without any excuse.

This three-fold change runs to the core of our beings. It has soaked through to the center. **"The heart is ... desperately wicked; Who can know it?"** (Jeremiah 17:9.) No wonder Isaiah portrays our absolute best as quite worthless.

"... all our righteousnesses are like filthy rags" (Isaiah 64:6). Our wickedness, not our attempted good, is equated with "filthy rags." And how much can we do to effect a change by ourselves? Nothing! **"Can the Ethiopian change his skin or the leopard its spots? Then may you also do good who are accustomed to do evil"** (Jeremiah 13:23).

We are sinful by nature and by choice, and we cannot help either, on our own.

B. Change in Leadership.

In ancient times, the goal in battle was to get to the opposite king. Once he was killed or captured, the battle was effectively over—it was won. The enemy was now fit to be enslaved. This world's rulership was given to Adam at the outset, when God said, **"...Have dominion..."** (Genesis 1:28). When Adam yielded to temptation and obeyed Satan rather than God, he was "captured." He surrendered his God-given authority to Satan, who immediately grabbed the kingship and claimed to be head. Later, when he met Jesus in the wilderness, he **"... showed Him all the kingdoms of the world in a moment of time.... And said ... this *has been delivered* to me, and I give it to whomsoever I wish"** (Luke 4:5, 6). This rulership was delivered to Satan by the first pair: **"...you are that one's slaves whom you obey..."** (Romans 6:16).

Adam and Eve obeyed Satan and brought their entire progeny—"all the kingdoms of the world"—under his jurisdiction and into sin's bondage.

Our fallen nature and enslavement to Satan made the grip of sin on humans unbreakable, permanent, and fatal! What remained in the hands of humans was the choice to cry out for help, but they were left without the power to break the vice-like grip.

1. The Conditions for Return to Paradise.

Include a) Full payment for sin,and b) perfect conformity to God's rules.

a. Full Payment.

The payment was life. **"The wages of sin is death"** (Romans 6:23). **"The soul who sins shall die"** (Ezekiel 18:4). We do not possess any extra life to fall back on or to share with others who may have forfeited theirs. If the punishment were a jail term or a fine or some community service, we could pay the price and then carry on in life. But the fee was life itself.

The dues were not optional. They were "wages" to be relentlessly exacted, and once remitted, would arrest life, making the return to paradise completely out of the question.

b. Perfect Conformity.

Even if full payment could have been made, there was still the condition of living a life of perfect conformity to the standard, failing which, there would be another payment to be made. But the corrupted nature and its enslavement precluded the possibility of living anywhere near that standard.

So all we could do was pile up a debt of death upon death, ad infinitum! And no way out was available: every door was shut, with not a sliver of hope anywhere.

This realization does not come by constantly defending our behavior, prestige, or character. It comes by being quietly reflective, honestly evaluating ourselves as to what we know to be our duty to ourselves, to others, and to God. Sadly, it appears that most religionists, including Christians, have missed the focus. They think that searching for and getting to the right rule or philosophy or religion (which they call "truth"), and then simply implementing it, will suffice. But that "truth" cannot be "euangelion" to one who is crippled and unable to perform. When are we going to become frank and truthful enough to confess that we are nowhere near the mark—not even the one we have set for ourselves? The added realization of how much we can do to salvage the situation elicits the hopeless, despairing cry, **"Who will deliver me from this body of death?"** (Romans 7:24.)

If it is such a universal phenomenon, why doesn't everybody acknowledge it and immediately go looking for a solution? The Bible gives a reason. It depicts us as being tricked by sin.

Temperature regulation is a finely tuned mechanism in the body. When the limits of the narrow range are crossed, measures are immediately activated to bring the temperature back to normal. But sometimes, when the temperature goes to extremes, the regulatory mechanisms themselves are disabled, leaving the counter-measures immobilized. Such a condition becomes a medical emergency, because the body has now become defenseless. The extreme change produced a condition in which the body, with all its finely tuned mechanisms, was "tricked" into a false sense of security. It could neither sense the correct condition, nor do anything about it. The only hope at that point is to bring in measures from outside the body to reverse the change.

Sin is a deception: **"Sin... deceived me"** (Romans 7:11); **"the deceitfulness of sin..."** (Hebrews 3:13). The heart that is wicked (sinful) is **"deceitful above all things. Who can know it?"** (Jeremiah17:9).

The condition produced benumbs the alerting mechanisms, and sin cannot be recognized as harmful. Now, it is welcomed as something which it really is not—a path to liberty and ultimate pleasure. Neither is it shunned as the deadly principle that it really is—a ruthless destroyer. We are no longer able to discern sin's true nature or sense the gravity of the condition. The only hope is to bring in measures from "outside."

So here is the picture. We are sinful by nature and by choice. We are enslaved under the jurisdiction of Satan, not able to live in conformity to God's will or to make payment for even one mistake. We do not recognize that such is our condition, and to top it all, we are deceived to the point of welcoming sin as desirable! I cannot think of any other combination that can produce a more desperate, hopeless, and incorrigible condition.

Against this background, the story of Jesus becomes "Euangelion"—Good News!

This Good News, which came from "outside," had to be preceded by a forerunner (also from an external source), the task of which was to prepare us to accept the Good News. It had to bring us to the point of recognizing our condition and countering the deception, to some degree. Nobody was going to look for a solution while unaware of the problem.

The first step was to establish a reference point or standard against which all of life could be compared. Called the Law (or Commandment), it was given by Jehovah God (the external Source) to Moses, on Mount Sinai. This was the forerunner.

The two most common responses to the Law are immediately to attempt to follow it or to discard it altogether. Those who attempt to follow it think that if they could but reach the standard, all would be well between themselves and God. Those who discard it see no relevance to it in their lives. But the Law was not given either to make us look good or to be thrown away. It was given for one important initial function—to show us our true condition, which was anything but good:

> **"...By the Law is the knowledge of sin ... that every mouth may be stopped and all the world may become guilty before God"** (Romans 3:19, 20); **"...the Law entered that the offense might abound"** (Romans 5:20); **"...so that sin through the commandment (Law) might become exceedingly sinful"** (Romans 7:13).

The Law was not given to show how virtuous and respectable we are but to establish the exact opposite—our total moral bankruptcy. But we will not realize it until we take the Law to be a changeless standard, attempt to follow it perfectly, and then honestly measure ourselves against both the letter and spirit of its tenets. Diligently done, it will lead to an inescapable conclusion—our condition is hopeless, deserving only of death:

> **"...When the commandment came, sin revived and I died. And the commandment which was to bring life, I found to bring death"** (Romans 7:9, 10).

But the Law does not abandon us. Once the initial function is accomplished, it pushes us toward a specific goal. **"Therefore the Law was our tutor to bring us to Christ ..."** (Galatians 3:24). In ancient times, the tutor was not the one who taught in school but was a hired hand whose main responsibility was to see that the children were chaperoned and shepherded all the way from home to school. They made sure that they reached the school and did not run off to play truant. They guided them to the correct destination. Once the Law is accepted as the standard, it becomes a mirror and faithfully reflects our true condition. Then, because it came from the same source as the Good News, it directs us, like a "tutor," to the solution. It does this in a unique way—by confessing that it is not the solution and that we had better look elsewhere for hope:

> **"... By the deeds of the law no flesh will be justified in His sight..."** (Romans 3:20); **"knowing that a man is not justified by the works of the law ..."** (Galatians 2:16); **"... no one is justified by the law in the sight of God..."** (Galatians 3:11).

In other words, the attempt to comply with the standard and so get our life record endorsed and approved of God (thus justifying ourselves), simply does not work. The inclination to show ourselves upright and commend ourselves is so strong that these tough, uncompromising statements become essential. Having nowhere else to go, we are now turned on our heels to the only option left—asking the Giver of the Law if there is any suggestion He might have. And does He have one to make!

The Good News

This, He was waiting to offer all along. He gives not just a suggestion but the ultimate solution, capable of dealing decisively with the whole spectrum of insurmountable obstacles facing humanity.

This ingenious plan was packaged and brought to us in the person of Jesus Christ. **"Look unto Me and be saved, all you ends of the earth"** (Isaiah 44:22). To look to, and within, humans for anything worthwhile was only futility. But this Man came onto the scene, and in the thick of the hopelessly one-sided battle, turned the tide eternally in favor of humanity. Euangelion!

But for it to be euangelion, it had to address and settle every hurdle. Leaving out even one would not provide any real solution. Running nearly twenty-six miles of a marathon but leaving out the last 100 yards would still be an incomplete performance, and the run would not be counted as a marathon.

The problem facing us was fourfold. Each aspect had to be overcome.

- Our corrupt nature
- Our alienation from God
- Full payment for all sin
- Living in full conformity to the will of God

Our Corrupt Nature

The corruption is so deep-rooted and total that it has no remedy. Not a chance in the world exists that it can be fixed and mended. The only way out is to kill it and have a new nature reborn.

Jesus told Nicodemus, a revered Pharisee, **"You must be born again"** (John 3:7), because the nature he was born with was simply unfixable.

Jesus took up this challenge in a unique way. He, God, became incarnate—

> **"... born of a woman, born under the law to redeem those who were under the law"** (Galatians 4:4, 5). **"Inasmuch then as the children have partaken of flesh and blood, he himself likewise shared in the same..."** (Hebrews 2:14).

At His incarnation, He was given a human body. This body contained the essence of humanity, and thus He became the representative of the whole human race. Whatever He would do would be credited to the whole race. In the last Olympics in China one of their divers, a petite little athlete, won her event. The news reported it the next day as "China gets the gold." Did the population of China, over one billion strong, take part in the diving event? Of course not! Their representative won, and all the one billion got the credit and the glory. Every Chinese could proudly smile at having won the gold medal.

> **"A body You have prepared for Me.... In the volume of the Book it is written of Me.... to do Your will, O God"** (Hebrews 10:5, 7, quoted from Psalm 40:6-8).

That which humanity could not do—live a life of perfect conformity to God's will—Jesus in His human body did. He took our nature, and in a real-life battle, put it to death. One of its decisive confrontations took place in the wilderness soon after His baptism. There, He met the full force of sin's temptations as they were flung at Him—and won. Corruption in human nature was given a death blow.

When He won, all humanity could claim the victory. The headlines could read, "Humanity Wins Battle."

> **"All heaven triumphed in the full and entire victory He had gained in behalf of man."** E. G. White, *Selected Messages,* bk. 1 (Washington, D.C.: Review and Herald Publishing Association, 1958 and 1980), p. 289.

In Jesus, the ultimate end to corruption in human nature was assured.

Our Alienation From God

A break occurred in the relationship between the first pair and God, when they yielded to Satan and allowed the principle of sin to dominate. This principle, at variance with God, caused complete disharmony. The friendship was marred, and the couple had to leave the Garden of Eden, showing that the return to Eden (paradise) would require a reversal of what had taken place. When Jesus defeated the principle of sin, bearing Deity and humanity in Himself, the barrier was broken down, and the Godly principles in control could connect humans with God again. **"God was in Christ reconciling the world to Himself"** (2 Corinthians 5:18). Thus, the estrangement between humanity and God was dissolved, and the connection reestablished.

> **"He [Jesus] took in His grasp the world over which Satan claimed to preside as his lawful territory and by His wonderful work in giving His life, He restored the whole race of men back to favor with God"** (White, *Selected Messages,* bk. 1, p. 343).

The reconciliation was not only a change in standing but a change in their attitude, too. Now the heart began to love God's ways and realized that following all the laws and rules of God would constitute the highest joy and greatest pleasure. It would lead to the truth that freedom lies not in the pattern of breaking the rules and suffering the consequences, but in the *other pattern* of keeping to them and reaping the rewards. Now the mind would begin to resonate in the same frequency as the mind of God.

Payment for Sin

All fair judicial actions require, as their basis, payment for the crime. Crimes against a kingdom are not light matters and are called treason. Sin is a crime against God's kingdom. The effects and repercussions are devastating. If ever the guilty should be forgiven, justice would demand full payment.

Jesus came from the realm of the infinite. His life measured with eternity. The smallest insult/humiliation or sacrifice would translate to infinite insult/humiliation—infinite sacrifice. What Jesus went through was anything but small. The horrendous sufferings of Gethsemane and the cross were the worst that could have been inflicted. In that dreadful experience, He went to the extreme and surrendered His life as a sacrifice, for the sake of humanity. As such, it was an infinite payment—"a sacrifice that would be efficacious to cleanse all—even the most sinful and degraded" and be sufficient to cover any sum of finite sins of any magnitude. The worst of our sins are more than covered by that payment. Was this a fair transaction? He accomplished **"our salvation in a way satisfactory to the demands of God's justice and consistent with the elevated holiness of His law." "What right had Christ to take the captives out of the enemy's hands? The right of having made a sacrifice that satisfies the principles of justice by which the kingdom of heaven is governed"** (E. G. White, *Selected Messages*, bk. 1, p. 309). The debt of the whole race was cleared!

Yes, there are conditions to the application of this emancipation, when it comes to the individual, because personal choice cannot be arbitrarily thrust aside in a just and fair process. But no condition can reduce the magnitude and grandness of this feat. It affected the whole human race and permanently removed the fear of judgment and death from *anyone* who decided to choose Him.

Full Conformity to God's Will

> **"Fifteen million minutes of life on this earth, in the midst of a wicked and corrupt generation—every thought, every deed, every purpose, every work, privately and publicly, from the time He opened His baby eyes until He expired on the cross, were all approved of God. Never once did our Lord have to confess sin, for He had no sin"** (Wilbur Smith, quoted in NEDV, p. 311).

Numerous times, temptations came in full, blinding force, but Jesus never wavered. We give in, and the temptation eases off for the moment. We have not gone the distance to bear the full strength of all the temptations we face. But **"... consider Him who endured such hostility.... You have not yet resisted to bloodshed striving against sin"** (Hebrews 12: 3, 4).

He went the full distance each time. The test for full conformity was brought to a head in the Garden of Gethsemane. Here was the one time in His life when He paused. The test was piercing and appeared too painful to bear. The record confesses that He pleaded for a way out. **"Oh, My Father, if it is possible, let this cup pass from Me"** (Matthew 26:39). But the final choice was one of submission to God's will: **"... Nevertheless, not as I will, but as You will"** (Matthew 26:39). That submission capped the only life in history lived in full conformity to the will of God.

This record can be credited to the human race, because He performed that incredible feat as a human and for humans.

The Bible describes our natural birth as being "in Adam" and the change to the new life as being "in Christ." So we were "in Adam" at our birth and were placed "in Christ" at His incarnation. Both were done without our choices. Therefore, both become ultimately void till a choice is made.

The people before the times of Jesus looked forward, trusting that He would come and accomplish their salvation, and those who did so were to be counted "in Christ" once the transaction was completed. Those after His time look back to that same life, trusting that the gift of being included among the saved would apply to them personally too, and if they did so, they were counted "in Christ." So, people "in Adam," both before and after, have a way of being incorporated "in Christ," and it is attained by a simple and whole-hearted choice.

It is an individual, private matter, and the choice is free. No amount of outward coercion, cajoling, or bribery has any effect here. While these may lead to an outward expression of assent, the issue here takes place in the depths of the heart, where fair play is governed by God Himself. No mistakes exist here. The most pious may turn out to be a traitor from deep within, and the worst sinner may make it to the kingdom of God, if the inner choice was real.

When we use this freedom of choice and opt for Jesus, there is an experience that comes attached with it called "being born again." Not just a warm, fuzzy feeling or some weird, unusual, unexplained encounter, this includes a complete change of status that truly, and in cosmic, legal terms, shifts you into a new family, based on putting to death the corrupt nature and re-birth to the new God-like nature. All this is done first in the person of Jesus Christ and then credited and applied, in real-life terms to **"whosoever believes"** (John 3:16); **"... if anyone is in Christ, he is a new creation"** (2 Corinthians 5:17).

This cannot be found "in Adam" (our natural birth), so to look for it in our own selves will be futile. **"He [God] has made us accepted *in the Beloved*"** (Ephesians 1:6). We are not acceptable on our own. Paul described all the high-sounding credentials bestowed through his pedigree, but valued them as **"rubbish, that I may gain Christ and be found *in Him*..."** (Philippians 3:8, 9). Why? Because being "in Adam" is being in a fatal state, while being "in Jesus" is being safe.

He dealt decisively and permanently with all our problems:

- Our corrupt natures
- Our alienation from God
- Our payment for sins
- Our requirement of full conformity to God's will

That which had spelled devastation, ruin, and death had been successfully and eternally solved in Him. Good News!

Not only did He settle the problems, but in so doing, He brought life, abundance, and a great and real hope of heaven.

> **"He who hears My words and believes on Him who sent Me ... has passed from death to life"** (John 5:24).

> **"I have come that they may have life and that they may have it *more abundantly*"** (John 10:10).

> **"A living hope ... to an inheritance incorruptible and undefiled and that does not fade away, *reserved* in heaven for you"** (1 Peter 1:3, 4).

"Reserved" by a Title and signed by a "DEED"—Calvary! And it is all ours, if we but believe and accept it whole-heartedly.

To the one who has realized his own true condition and has cried out in despair from the depths for help and relief, this Man comes as "Euangelion! And Euangelion again!"

18

The Supreme Transaction

Because of the way some terms will be used in this chapter, they will have to be defined or described, for the sake of clarity. These definitions/descriptions are not set and fixed, by any means; in fact, they are ones that I have tried to outline so that the picture I would like to portray becomes evident.

Justice: This requires an unalterable reference point—a rule or law. To this are attached the consequences of compliance or non-compliance—rewards or punishments—which also are unchangeable. If any of these three—rule, reward, or retribution—are tampered with and changed, the process becomes arbitrary and is no longer justice. Nor can it be maintained, if the magnitude of the crime is ignored; hence, the idea of "An eye for an eye and a tooth for a tooth."

We often think of this as being inhuman and barbaric, a primitive exacting of revenge. But on careful consideration, it appears the highest form of justice. "An eye for a tooth" or "a life for a finger" would be sheer injustice. Justice requires equity—one to be exactly equal to the other. The whole of jurisprudence is based on this principle. All the myriad laws, codes, sections, subsections, amendments, and caveats have been described with a singular focus—to make things fair and equal. That is the foundation of justice.

But if justice is the only basis of a relationship, it will sound the death-knell to it, and life will become unbearable or cease altogether. No one can claim to have been given all the rewards and all the punishments deserved by action, thought, and motive. Another factor exists that allows life to carry on, but maintains justice as well. Mercy accomplishes this, with forgiveness as one of its components and the key reason for its functioning.

Mercy: We often picture mercy as bending the rules to reduce a punishment, or benignly saying "It's OK." But mercy cannot change the rule, reward, or retribution, for that would be tampering with justice. In its ultimate sense, it is allowed expression on only one point—to *whom* the reward goes or from whom the retribution is demanded. Justice is satisfied, as long as the axe falls. Mercy, while it cannot stop it from falling, can decide where it falls. Justice, like a cannon, is satisfied as long as it fires. Mercy, unable to stop the blast, is allowed to influence the process by changing the direction of the fire. Justice is not violated, as long as the dues are paid. Mercy decides who should make the payment, but full payment must be made. If the rule, reward, or retribution is changed one iota, justice flies out the window, and there will be no need for mercy. Arbitrariness will hold sway, and there will be neither justice nor mercy.

Can mercy blindly or forcibly pick the new recipient? No, there is still a requirement to be fulfilled. The new recipient should be fully aware of all the consequences and should voluntarily accept the deal. Coercion would constitute injustice. Mercy can retain its quality only if justice retains *its* qualities and remains inflexible and utterly changeless. Mercy is, at the point of final reckoning, dues for one's actions, paid in full by another. Only in this way can justice remain intact, while allowing the guilty to be forgiven completely.

Righteousness/Holiness: These words sound archaic and reminiscent of medieval saints and bishops. The first picture that comes to mind is of an ascetic, deep in meditation and far removed from the "pleasures" of this world—or of a priest dedicated to celibacy and fasting, with the earnestness showing as a halo 'round his head. Something is almost mysterious, unapproachable, and even nebulous about it. Since we are unable to define it, we may become uncomfortable with it. But it is a major Christian concept.

The meaning of the word *righteous* is doing something "right" or "correctly," so that the required standard is met. But apparent good can be done with a bad plan, and a good action with a correct plan can be done from a wrong motive. It appears, then, that we live on three levels: 1) actions, which are based on 2) plans and schemes, which are driven by 3) motives—and the crux seems to be the motive. Motives form the springboard of all that we undertake. Perfect actions and plans are still not acceptable, if the motive prompting them was bad. And mistakes in actions and plans are tolerated, if the motive was good.

What makes the motive acceptable or unacceptable, good or evil, righteous or unrighteous? Cutting off the trimmings, I believe we can come to a concise core concept. Simply put, righteousness is the principle of "You first—not I." Faced with a choice in any given situation, I place the other on a higher priority than myself. Anything that benefits me will not provide any sense of satisfaction, till I know that the other has been served first. All "good"' behavior rests on this foundation.

In a sense, this is a description of love. God is righteous. God is also love. He doesn't have to choose to love. While He can choose to express that love in a hundred ways, He does not have to make up His mind about love. He cannot help but love, because that is His essence, His nature, and His substance. Water cannot keep from wetting what it touches. That which cannot wet is not water. The color red cannot exist outside its wavelength. That which exhibits another wavelength will no longer be red. Similarly, God cannot do anything other than love He possesses only that quality and exists only in that "wavelength." What is the nature of that love? Some of the haziness rests in the fact that the word *love* has many meanings. The Greeks help us out some. Their language utilizes different words to show the various shades of meaning and the differing relationships in which it is expressed.

- *Eros* is romantic, passionate love, in which physical intimacies play a major role and which is best exemplified in marriage.
- *Fileo* is the love among family members. Devotion and a sense of belonging form a large part in that relationship.
- *Sturges* is love expressed among friends. Platonic, it has loyalty as its mark.
- *Caritas* involves the willingness and desire to help, especially those in need.
- *Agape* is the Christian concept of Godly love. Its primary expression is self-forgetfulness and seeking the best for the other person.

A basic difference exists between agape and the other types. All the others are human forms and can be generated within our experience. Agape is superhuman and has to be supplied from a source outside us. The greater difference, however, is that while all human types require an incentive or reason for their expression, agape *needs no reason.* Eros requires attraction. Fileo requires family. Sturges requires friendship. Caritas requires a condition that elicits sympathy. Agape can love without any attraction, family ties, friendship, or feelings of sympathy. It can love the unlovely and is the only love that can "love your enemies," going to any lengths, if need be. When all the other forms of love have found their reasons to leave, agape remains. *It had no reason to be there in the first place; thus, it can find no reason to leave!* To have this as the motive, the innermost compulsion for all thoughts and actions, is true righteousness.

Unrighteousness/Sin: Once again, a rock-bottom definition—"Me first—not you." The essence of "badness"—it's the principle of placing oneself first and holding everyone else to a secondary or worse position. However "good" the actions and plans, if they are based on this principle, they remain in the category of unrighteousness.

Heaven: I believe the reason heaven is described in terms of gold, gems, and abundance of material things is because of our sense of values. Our minds are clouded, and we cannot clearly discern true values. We have failed to grasp the essence of life and have shifted our values from persons to things. The most valuable possession is not found in a treasure chest of diamonds but in the wonder and beauty of a heart-to-heart relationship. People and personal relationships create all the values of life. Can a diamond or a pearl take the place of a lover? Never! Nothing can ever replace that relationship! Neither the gold, nor the abundance of the place, makes it heaven. What makes it so is the presence of a Person—God—the most captivating and desirable Being in the universe. The close, loving relationship can give a restfulness and pleasure that is beyond words. Nothing else comes even close. Yes, there may be gold and precious gems there, but they do not constitute heaven, at its core. Jesus described the togetherness of that place in John 14:3:

> **"That where I am there you may be also."** One of the pictures of heaven, in the last book of the Bible, is: **"He will dwell *with them* and they shall be His people, and God Himself will be *with them* and be their God"** (Revelation 21:3.)

When two humans realize this and forge closeness, it becomes heaven on earth—the best we can have on this planet. When a human being and God reach an open, unbroken state of communion, it will be heaven. When it is in the realm of God, between God and God (Father and Son), it is the ultimate experience of bliss, in keeping with the degree of harmony that exists between them.

Hell: Here again, the focus must shift from the fire, burning sulfur, and scalded skin, to the pain of a broken relationship. Fire can burn the skin to cause pain, but pain from a broken relationship runs to the depths of the heart. Hell may contain fire, but the suffering is not primarily the heat; rather, it is the sense of eternal loss, a painful void that nothing can even begin to assuage. No pain can equal that of being torn away from a fond lover.

A ceremony was once practiced, but is now banned, in India, called "sati." When the husband died, the wife was to voluntarily jump into the funeral pyre and burn to death, rather than to go on living without her mate. Widespread as a practice in those days, many of these acts were truly voluntary! "Sati" showed that fire was more tolerable than separation from a loved one. Hell is a place where the relationship with God is permanently shattered.

When two humans break their relationship and become vicious enemies, it is hell on earth—the worst we can experience on this planet. When a human and God finally turn their faces away from each other permanently, it will be hell. When God is torn apart from God, it is the ultimate experience of pain and suffering—worse than hell—and goes beyond word or imagination.

Death: The Bible describes two deaths. The first death is described in terms of the consequence of the principle of sin in our existence. Temporary and universal, it is not related to the ultimate choice regarding good and evil. From this, a resurrection will take place.

The second death (Revelation 20:6) appears to be the punishment for our final decision to retain the principle of sin in our lives; it is permanent and inflicted only on those who have made that settled but wrong choice.

Suffering of Death: Hebrews 2:9 uses the words *suffering of death.* It seems that this suffering occurs while its victim is still alive. Suffering ceases once death supervenes. If it is related to the second death, it is the sense of impending eternal doom; the excruciating pain and sinking feeling when facing a permanent separation from God, in a hopelessly severed relationship—it is the suffering of hell!

And now, on to the narrative.

We pick it up in a garden on a Thursday night. The Passover meal has been eaten. Jesus and His disciples have reached the Garden of Gethsemane. The moon shines full, and the air is still. But the apparent calm belies an internal storm, for He is in deep anguish as He stumbles along, as if under a staggering burden. Then, unable to hold His balance, He falls to the ground. His fingers claw the raw earth, as His quivering lips part in an agonizing plea, "Oh, my Father, is there no other way? The pain runs too deep. I feel ripped apart. No more, please!"

What is happening here? Isn't this the Man who had commanded the storm into subjection; who had ordered the demons around, making them beg at His feet; who had spoken life into a corpse? Had faith and fortitude finally failed Him? Was He being a coward, running away from known duty and now whimpering just because it got too close for comfort?

Compare this with John Huss at the stake, or the maidens in the coliseums of first-century Rome. There, it was customary for the fire to be lighted behind the one tied to the stake. But Huss called out to the torchbearer, "Come light the fire before my face. If I was afraid, I would not have been here!" When the maidens and little children were thrown to the lions, they would form a circle, hold hands, and sing, "Unto Him who loved us and washed us in His blood," as those hungry beasts charged across the arena to tear them to pieces. Why could Jesus not brace up to what was confronting Him? Why was He not singing?

Mel Gibson's movie *The Passion of the Christ* seems to have caught some of the torture that Jesus went through.

Deep-seated hatred was on display. The Jews and Romans hated one another with a passion. But when it came to Jesus, so great was their hatred toward Him that they were willing to make a temporary alliance to pour out their combined hatred against Him.

Shame—physical, social, and moral shame—was heaped on Jesus. Artists paint a loincloth around His waist. But usually, those crucified were hung up stark naked! This was done to strip away every last vestige of dignity from such base criminals. The type of torture itself signified the vileness of the person. To the Jew, hanging was the incontrovertible sign of the curse of God, as established in the Books of Law. Nothing was more shameful than this.

Christ also experienced physical suffering of immense magnitude. The flogging; the gouged-out skin and flesh; the spikes going through joints and ligaments; the dislocated shoulders; the burning thirst; and finally, the slow, lingering suffocation lasting from three to seven days that brought the miserable process to a close—all these made death dearer than life to the tortured.

Most point to these, when speaking of the cross that brought salvation to the human race. But if the hatred, the shame, and the physical suffering were all that the story was telling, Jesus should have been able to face them all boldly and go through them singing. There appears to be more to it.

Jesus did not come just to be tortured on a cross. He came to pay the price to procure salvation for you and me, and if the things we have mentioned bought salvation, then we must presume that Satan, along with Pilate, the Jewish priests, and the Roman soldiers, joined hands with God for that great rescue act. But there was no cooperation between God and them. Satan was not working out any salvation—only God was. Things happened at the same time and place, but the events were worlds apart. The cross, the nails, the thorns, the spear, did not procure anybody's salvation.

So, what did?

The story began before the Creation of the world. Jesus is described as **"the Lamb slain from the foundation of the world"** (Revelation 13:8). If the description takes us that far back, there must have been a provision made before the world began. I have come to appreciate it and call it "The Primary Covenant." Scholars portray the relationship between humans and God in terms of two covenants/contracts. They call them the First and Second, or the Old and the New, or the Mosaic and the Abrahamic, or the Old Dispensation and the New Dispensation. The First places the burden of performance on humans; the Second allows God to do the main performing. These are contracts between God and humans.

The Primary Covenant is not one between God and humans but between members of the Godhead—God the Father, God the Son, and God the Holy

Spirit. Before Creation, they met together and, clasping hands, entered into a binding oath which stated that should humans falter and forfeit life, they would be brought back to the path of life at any cost to themselves. This, I believe, is the covenant/contract that saves and which uses the other two as tools in the process.

The Covenant required that one of them become a human. The Son of God volunteered. In becoming human, He could not stop being God. That would be impossible. What He did was to lay aside all the rights and prerogatives of God and live in the wisdom, strength, and moral ability of a human. But the essence of humanity (through Adam) had already failed and was now subject to sin and corruption. If He was to become that type of a human, how would He live above the power of sin and not sink under its weight and power? A possible solution was available. He would not live by the power of His own divinity or by the inherent qualities of His humanity. The first would be unfair and untruthful—His pretending to be human, while not being truly, wholly human. The second would be to invite defeat, with its disastrous results! Rather, He would live as a human, possessing those qualities but denying them by choice and depending on the strength, wisdom, and moral ability that His Father would supply on a moment-to-moment basis.

That is why He declared, **"I can of myself do nothing"** (John 5:30). He went so far as to confess that even the words that He spoke were from the Father: **"The Father who sent Me gave Me a command, what I should say and what I should speak"** (John 12:49). Every statement, every truth, every doctrine, every parable, every miracle, every answer to those artful, scheming Pharisees, was because of total dependence on the Father. No wonder He spent whole nights in prayer—chalking out the course for each day, each trial, one at a time. Nothing that He did was without His Father's express permission and by the wisdom and power the Father granted Him.

In return, His Father was His never-failing, absolutely dependable, unfaltering source of everything He needed. Nobody could fool Him, trick Him, trip Him up, or make Him jealous or hateful, so long as He was in contact with His Father. Nobody could harm Him—He was protected by the Father Himself. Satan and the people tried to get at Him, beginning from Herod, but no one could, because **"His hour had not come"** (John 7:30; 8:20).

Then something happened the evening of Thursday that changed the whole picture. The previous, confident affirmations gave way to, **"This is your hour and the power of darkness"** (Luke 22:53).

"For this purpose I came to this hour" (John 12:27). **"He began to**

be sorrowful and deeply distressed. ... 'My soul is exceedingly sorrowful, even to death'" (Matthew 26:37, 38.) **"And His sweat became like great drops of blood falling to the ground"** (Luke 22:44).

Why this dramatic, frightful transformation?

A major paradigm shift, a huge change of standing and purpose, had taken place. He who was earlier called the "Lion of Judah" was now becoming a submissive sacrifice as the "Lamb of God." In the Jewish sacrificial system, the first requirement of the lamb was to become a sin-bearer. So on Him who had never sinned, who had never known the experience in His heart, was laid every sin from Adam to the last one who will ever live. Some imagine it as being like a burden placed on the head or shoulders, or like a garment that was wrapped around Him. But no, the record is shocking—**He was *made* "to *be* sin for us"** (2 Corinthians 5:21).

He did not just take on our sin—He *became* our sin! The time had come to deal with sin, and on that fateful Friday, hanging there forsaken and alone, it was gathered up in one life-choking heap and placed on this Man. On that day, the sins of the whole human race were found on that center cross! He was "delivered up" (Romans 4:25), not to the Jewish priests or to Pilate or to the Roman soldiers, but to the full and final punishment of sin. God, and full-blown rebellion, which sin really is, cannot co-exist. Action was imperative; one or the other would have to give way. Here, no angel, demon, or human has the authority to act. A law had been violated, and only the Maker of that law could respond and punish. **"We esteemed Him stricken, smitten by *God* and afflicted"** (Isaiah 53:4). God, the Author of the Law, was dealing with it. He must punish to the full extent that the Law demanded, and send the Sin-bearer off to that God-forsaken, God-abandoned place and experience called Hell! This constituted the central act of the mercy of God. Justice demanded the falling of the axe. Mercy directed that it fall on Jesus.

The separation between sin and righteousness, between the Son and the Father, began in Gethsemane, and how Jesus' heart loathed it! **"My soul is exceedingly sorrowful, even unto death"** (Matthew 26:38). The story pictures Him clinging to the earth and rocks, as He felt Himself dragged away from His Father.

And here is the fundamental difference between Jesus and every other martyr down through the ages. God was there beside the martyrs. The Father's sustaining, comforting presence was right there. With Him alongside, courage and music could remain. But when the lifeline to God is fractured, *no one* can sing—not even the Son of God! No one can sing when facing hell—for the source of the song itself has vanished! We get a small glimpse of the agony of that prayer—"Let this cup pass from Me. The pain runs too deep, My Father." Sometime in Gethsemane and after, the Father fell silent. The contact was being broken, and the process worsened hour after tormenting hour.

"Father, will I be able to come through this all right?" Silence.

"Will I really rise the third day? Only on Your word did I speak so boldly. Now, I need Your reassurance."

Silence.

"Trusting You, I spoke boldly about my resurrection. I need reassurance now. Just one word, Father, and it will be enough. Do not abandon Me now."

Silence.

Then, as the full realization came crashing in—that this was the judgment of a fully truthful and righteous God against sin; this was the sentence to which there could be no repeal; this was a one-way street marked "No Return!"—wrung from those parched, pale, quivering lips came the bitterest cry this universe will ever hear—**"Eloi, Eloi, lama sabachthani?"**

"My God, My God, have You forsaken Me?"

"Now, when I need You the most, where are You?"

No fire or burning sulfur, no cross or nails, no thorn or spear can match this anguish, this agony of soul-separation between Father and Son! This is the cry of the heart when the abandonment has been utter; when the cannon of justice points but there is no mercy to divert it (because all that there was of mercy had been exhausted for us). This is the cry of the soul sinking into hell itself!

In the midst of that superhuman agony came one last, stinging temptation. The priests and rabbis were there to watch the finale of their concerted moves. With voices full of haughtiness and sarcasm, they taunted, "You said You were the Son of God. Do You feel like it now? Let's make a deal. Come down from the cross, and we will believe that You are the Son of God." They did not even know what that challenge meant. How much like us today! They asked for a miracle so that they could believe, yet right before them was the greatest miracle of all. For which is greater—to come down, if it were possible, or to stay dangling there in torturous pain, out of sheer love! They did not know that He hung there *because* He was the Son of God. To come down would have been to deny His mission and the very fabric of His character—and to prove the exact opposite!

He could have come down. The writing says He went to the cross voluntarily. But for whom was He dying, anyway? His nation had rejected Him. The religious leaders in His community had actively plotted to kill Him and had gone to the extent of courting the Romans to get it done. All His disciples had fled. One had betrayed Him, and another—one of the closest—had denied having anything to do with Him, cursing and swearing to emphasize it. For whom was He dying? How dark and hopeless the prospect of making the ultimate sacrifice, with nothing to show and nobody at all to benefit from it!

He could have come down, but He stayed there.

The cross, at its core, was a choice—a simple, single, piercing choice—"Save Yourself—or save this world of ungrateful, blundering wretches." Did a choice really exist? On the one hand, the Majesty of heaven, the beloved Prince of the angelic host—and on the other, corrupt, hateful, ruthless self-seekers such as you and I. How difficult was it to make that choice? But love and righteousness, like evil and sin, cannot be explained. Sin with a reason is not sin anymore. Love with a reason is not love anymore. Both are, alike, complete mysteries.

Watch as He contemplates the choice and then settles onto one side. What tilted the balance? I believe there was one factor—my face and yours. He saw us, 2,000 years later, all bruised and battered in life; weak and woeful; hopelessly and helplessly sliding down a slippery slope straight to perdition and hell. And in His great heart rose up a wondrous compassion for us—so deep and great that He forgot about Himself. If He did not go through with it, we would be lost, and He did not want to let us go. So in one of the clearest and most brilliant demonstrations of righteousness ever witnessed, He turned to us and said, "You first—not I." And then: "If that is the choice, Father, My mind is made up. Give them a chance for heaven, where We have lived from eternity in pure bliss. As for Me, 'Good-bye forever.'"

Somewhere along in the hours, as He hung on the cross, the Father cut Himself off completely from the Son, in an act of consummate justice against sin; and with that severance went the hope of His own resurrection. He could not see beyond the tomb.

He died with you and me, not Himself, on His mind. God—and God—had been torn apart! God and God had suffered to the ultimate degree. And They had done it voluntarily. Today, in contemplation, I exclaim, "What wondrous love is this, oh my soul!" **"In this is love, not that we loved God, but that *He* loved us …"** (1 John 4:10). This "love" is *agape*—that which cannot find a reason to stop expressing itself, and so remains, even to the point of death.

But come the third day, He rose up, according to the Book. How? Why?

Jesus belonged to the realm of God, and therefore, of infinity. Any insulting treatment given Him, however small, would translate to an infinite insult. Any discomfort or pain becomes infinite in nature and magnitude. What He went through was anything but small or petty. The horrendous "suffering of death" was an infinite price—sufficient to pay for every sin. The ultimate Judge was satisfied that justice had been rendered. **"He shall see the travail of His soul, and be *satisfied*"** (Isaiah 53:11).

Since He had paid the price but had never sinned in His own life, permitting Him to come back to life would still uphold justice. When His Father called Him back from the abyss of darkness and death, He came up from the grave in triumph over it, with life that, in His divinity, was His own—original, unborrowed, and underived—but it would be with an eternal difference. He had sacrificed it, and now He could not possess it all by Himself. He would have to share it with the ones for whom He had sacrificed it—with **"whosoever believes"** (John 3:16). The sweep of those words takes in every human who has ever lived or ever will live.

Romans 8:29 describes Him as "the firstborn." Before the cross, He was the *Only*; after the cross, He was the firstborn "among many brethren." The siblings are you and I! Hebrews 2:11 pictures the Sanctifier (God) and the sanctified (humans) as being of one stock, one family—blood relatives! After the resurrection, Jesus said, **"Go to My brethren and say to them, 'I am ascending to My Father and your Father, and to My God and your God'"** (John 20:17).

"The family of heaven and the family of earth are one." E. G. White, *The Desire of Ages* (Mountain View, CA: Pacific Press Publishing Association, 1940), p. 835.

This was the transaction that obtained salvation for you and me.

Reverie

Christianity is not primarily a set of doctrines and rules, although those are present. In its finest essence, it is the message about (and from) a Man who claimed to be God but who did not relish the position and powers of God while we were without hope—and who bore every insult and torture to bring us the chance of being adopted into His own family and having eternal life. Nobody ever, from such a height, went to such depths, to offer so much to so many!

> **"He arose from the tomb enshrouded with a cloud of angels in wondrous power and glory—the Deity and humanity combined. He took in His grasp the world over which Satan claimed to preside as his lawful territory, and by His wonderful work in giving His life, He restored the whole race of men to favor with God ..."** (E. G. White, *Selected Messages*, bk. 1 (Washington, D.C.: Review and Herald Publishing Association, 1958 and 1980), p. 343.

Accomplishment par excellence!

If the sins of the whole race were placed on Him, then, at some point, in some way, everyone is involved in this real-life drama.

Nobody is off-stage. This also means that the sins of everyone have been accounted for and dealt with. Imagine the relief and freedom to the one who whole-heartedly believes this—who believes that the ultimate Judge is willing to wipe off the whole debt from the account and offer a new, clean slate based on a forensic, legally sound argument—the debt has been fully paid, and the clean slate being offered was actually lived in real life in this Man! And it is free to everyone. There is no bar to receiving it, save our own personal choice.

This is why He came—to live life to perfection as a human and then to pay the full price for sin—all sin. This is why the most innocent (life lived to perfection) died the most horrible death (the ultimate price for sin). This unique plan upheld and satisfied justice as well as provided humans freedom from condemnation. It is offered as the only path of hope for us.

To the Godhead, the cost was tremendous—the event (Gethsemane and Calvary) to be borne only once in eternity.

> **"This sundering of the divine powers will never again occur throughout the eternal ages"** (E. G. White, *SDA Bible Commentary*, vol. 7, p. 924).

> **"Christ was offered once to bear the sins of many"** (Hebrews 9:28).

> **"For by one offering He has perfected forever those who are being sanctified"** (Hebrews 10:14).

Jesus was the Lamb of God—the One Supreme Sacrifice.

The extreme pain was borne by the Father, too. There was no way He could have escaped it.

> **"The omnipotent God suffered with His Son"** (E. G. White, *The Upward Look,* p. 223). **"God Himself was crucified with Christ; for Christ was one with the Father"** (E. G. White, *Signs of the Times,* March 26, 1894).

The Godhead was torn apart and experienced the "suffering of death"—an intensity of grief and pain that nothing can equal—to pay the cost. This sacrifice is what we are asked to accept.

This goes completely against the grain of how the relationship between humans and God is usually viewed. We think of humans bringing a sacrifice to God for His acceptance. Christianity is utterly unique—here, it is God who brings *His Sacrifice* to humans for acceptance! Is this not truly humbling? Yet it is the true picture of righteousness and agape, expressed to perfection in Jesus.

And once the Sacrifice is accepted in full belief, gratitude, springing from the heart, produces a willingness to please and obey God that no other power can possibly engender. The oath of loyalty becomes an inner compulsion. The relationship becomes the greatest treasure—not worth giving up, even in the face of death. That could be the reason why Christianity has produced more martyrs than any other single cause in history.

What if God brought *His Offering* to *you* for acceptance? What would be your response, dear reader?

My Response

MY RESPONSE

If this God was careful to preserve sufficient evidence to address my cold, questioning intellect; and if He left enough warmth and passion in the portrayal of His feelings toward me, to grip my wandering emotions,

then,

my response is from deep within—a place called "my heart"—that now feels safe to hang its eternal destiny on this Man,

Jesus,

whose story unfolds and is laid open in this Book—

the Bible.

—Subodh Pandit, M.D.

Section III

Appendices

Appendices

Appendix A: Evil, Suffering, and God

Of course, there is suffering and evil all around us. So what? It seemed too matter-of-fact to need any serious contemplation. I had taken it for granted that there would be an answer someday and that the apparent dilemma would somehow be solved. But later, as I came across deep, seasoned thinkers who had wrestled with the question, yet were unable to provide a satisfactory explanation, even to themselves, my complacency seemed naïve and simple.

Some seemed sure they had found a reasonable approach. Others confessed that they were foundering. Yet others decided simply to leave it as an open-ended question. Was it really such a difficult matter?

What caused the dilemma?

> **"Either He is not good or else He is not almighty"** (Epicurus, a Greek philosopher, 341 B.C.– 270 B.C.).

> **"Is he [God] willing to prevent evil, but unable? Then he is impotent. Is he able but not willing? Then he is malevolent. Is he both able and willing? Whence then is evil?"** David Hume, *Dialogues Concerning Natural Religion* (New York: Hafner, 1948), p. 66.

The problem was the difficulty in reconciling the existence of a loving, almighty God with the presence of evil and suffering, and this contradiction was of a magnitude sufficient to sway the minds of some thinkers and cause them to reject the idea of God altogether.

> **"The problem of evil is one of the most crucial protests raised by unbelievers against the fact of God."** James E. Orr, *The Faith That Persuades* (New York: Harper & Row, 1977), p. 80.

> **"Evil constitutes the *biggest single argument* against the existence of an almighty, loving God."** John W. Wenham, "Response," in Geisler, *The Roots of Evil* (Zondervan, 1978), p. 89.

> **"The *biggest single stumbling block* to belief in a God of love."** Ed L. Miller, *God and Reason, a Historical Approach to Philosophical Theology* (MacMillan, 1972), p, 139.

It appeared to be a huge, consequential question. And more than that, it seemed to be one of the most prevalent questions ever raised.

> **"It is a problem that no theist can avoid and no honest thinker will**

try to avoid." David E. Trueblood, *General Philosophy,* p. 226, quoted by Steve Kumar, *Christianity for Skeptics* (Peabody, MA: Hendrickson Publishers, 2000), p. 41.

"Indeed every philosophical theory has to deal with it in some way." R. C. Sproul, *Objections Answered* (Glendale, CA: GL Regal Books, 1978), p. 131.

"These are pressing questions which every reflective and sensitive mind frequently ponders" (Kumar, *Christianity for Skeptics,* p. 39).

What makes the problem particularly distressing is the fact that this abhorrent, unwelcome, unacceptable thing called evil brings pain, suffering, and injustice that are all too real. If only we could wipe it from our existence! But far from being destroyed; far from being pushed into a corner; it dominates our existence in such a ruthless, relentless manner that despair seems entirely reasonable. And because we are unable to do anything to alleviate it, the feeling of helplessness is utter. So when there is talk of a loving God who is also almighty and could have done something about it, the words sound hollow. They irk and taunt like a cruel joke. No wonder Stendhal is said to have declared:

"God's only excuse is that he does not exist" (quoted in Kumar, *Christianity for Skeptics,* p. 40). **"According to [Bertrand] Russell, no one could sit beside a dying child and still believe in the existence of God"** (Ibid.).

So here's the argument. Evil is real, horrendous, and unacceptable. We hate it but cannot do anything about it. We are totally helpless. In such circumstances comes the claim that there is a loving God, who is also powerful enough to have done something about it. But on observation, it seems obvious that He has decided not to do much to reduce the suffering around us. There is, therefore, a contradiction between God as being full of love, as well as His being all powerful, and it is so irreconcilable and vexing that the most reasonable conclusion is that God does not exist.

The argument is plausible but incomplete. At least two questions still need to be addressed.

1. Is "evil" the only factor to be considered?

2. Is this conclusion the only option we have?

Evil the Only Factor?

Is anything besides evil in our existence? The answer couldn't be more obvious: "Of course, there is!" On the other side of the spectrum are experiences that are equally undeniable. Joys, pleasures, and thrills are everywhere. Heroism, courage, and generosity still permeate our lives. Who can experience a mother's compassion, a father's self-sacrifice, a friend's loyalty and support, a lover's soft caress, and deny that there is fulfillment, security, and delight within reach, and sometimes, in fair measure? Stendhal and Russell would be wrong and quite out of touch with reality to deny these. A lot of good is in this world, too!

So why does the presence of good not raise a similar question regarding the existence of God? "Whence then is *good?*" In the name of equity and fairness, it should be conceded that if we have made a proposal that evil suggests the absence of God, the counter-proposal, that good suggests the presence of God, should be accepted as equally valid. If evil is the "most crucial protest," "the biggest single argument," "the biggest stumbling block" ***against*** the presence of God, then good should also form the "most crucial" argument and the "biggest single argument" ***for*** the presence of God! Atheism now becomes an untenable proposition, because it is forced to consider the existence of God as an equal alternative, since both evil and good are undeniable in our existence.

In this context, theism becomes justifiable, based on the reasoning that, within the same setting, evidence *for* a presence outweighs evidence *against* that presence, and thus defines the correct over-all picture. Lack of footprints in one part of the jungle, providing evidence against the presence of a lion, cannot negate the finding of footprints in another part, providing evidence *for* the presence of a lion. The final conclusion, taking the evidence in the whole jungle, should be that a lion is present. Similarly, in the setting of our existence, with evil as well as good being present, it is the evidence *for* the presence of God that must provide the final, correct picture of the whole setting.

While this does not resolve the conflict between the existence of a loving God and the presence of evil, it does restrain us from making that conflict an argument against the existence of God. In other words, the presence of evil does not, of itself, support atheism. It might have done so, if good had been completely absent. But such is just not the case.

Atheism the Only Possibility?

Admittedly, there is an apparent contradiction between God's love and power, especially when the presence of evil is also considered. But a contradiction does not give us the liberty to throw out both qualities, unless they are shown to be non-existent. What if you made a complaint of being pick-pocketed? Mr.

A blamed Mr. B for the deed, and vice versa. I, as the police officer, deliberating on it, said that since there were conflicting claims, the only way to resolve the matter was to declare that no one was pick-pocketed!

Wouldn't that be a travesty of fairness and justice? Even if the conflict were never resolved, such a conclusion would still not be warranted. Likewise, the contradiction between God's love and power does not prove that God is absent. Rather, it is only a description of what is—a contradiction, and nothing more.

In keeping with this, we should look for other possibilities, too. Along with atheism, there are three others, making a total of four.

1. God is evil.

2. God is good.

3. God is both good and evil.

4. God is non-existent.

The first is consistent with the evil in the world but contradicts the good.

The second is consistent with the good but contradicts the evil.

The third is usually found in mythological literature.

The fourth is a peculiar proposition. While it presents no obvious conflict, there is no explanation for the origin of either good or evil. If it did attempt one, the reasoning in section (A) would defeat it. To circumvent the hurdle, it evades both good and evil, treating them as if they did not exist, and takes two dubious approaches. First, it avoids making a counter-proposal. Second, it goes on to make a bizarre statement without bothering to provide any evidence for it whatsoever.

Absence of a Counter-proposal.

The proposal of theism includes the concept that God is "all in all" and so forms the ultimate reference point of our lives. He sets the criteria and standards for all evaluations.

Atheism does not make any clear-cut counter-proposal to this, although it probably does so by default. The default proposal should state that the *individual* is the ultimate reference point. This becomes an oxymoron, because there are now multiple reference points, each with a different idea of what constitutes "ultimate" authority. Therefore it cannot be "ultimate," in any sense of the word. In such circumstances, all claims should be given equal validity, even if they happen to be diametrically opposed to any other. Therefore, if there is a claim that God is the "ultimate" authority, it should be welcomed and accepted as candidly and as enthusiastically as its opposite claim. In other words, there is the distinct possibility that God exists. To deny this possibility is to deny the default counter-proposal (which allows this possibility), in which case, there will be no option but to accept the fact of God. So on approaching the question from either angle—that of the theistic proposal or that of the atheistic default proposal—the reality and relevance of God become inevitable.

This appears to be the reason why the atheistic argument stops short of making a real counter-proposal.

If it did, the possibility of the existence of God would become inevitable. And if that possibility is accepted, atheism becomes false!

The Atheistic Declaration

I still find myself shaking my head in disbelief at the absurdity of such a statement. When fair and honest arguments are not forthcoming as support, to resort to a declaration, by fiat, as it were, becomes a really pathetic cop-out. Here is the declaration: "There is, at bottom, no design, no purpose, no evil, and no good—nothing but blind, pitiless indifference."

The most basic and "crucial" argument used to make the case for atheism was that of the presence of evil. Now that the end has been gained, the argument is being disposed of. Can a foundation be demolished while retaining the superstructure? After using the main branch to get to the perch, the branch is nonchalantly chopped. What of the perch now? Evil is suddenly and arbitrarily chopped out of existence. What of the absence of God now?

"There is...no evil and no good..." Will anyone seriously agree with this? How patently false this statement is!

Yet, to be fair, let us examine it.

- "No evil" = Nothing is unacceptable = everything is acceptable = everything is good.
- "No good" = Nothing is acceptable = everything is unacceptable = everything is evil.

Each of these phrases should apply simultaneously, at all times, in all circumstances. So what is the real claim? NOT EVEN *NOTHING!* (With due respect to Steven Weinberg, Nobel Laureate and author of *Dreams of a Final Theory*. In describing conservatives, who claimed that there were absolutes, and liberals, who denied any such idea, he said that he happened to disagree with the conservatives on certain issues, but at least they were standing for something that could be discussed and probably shown to be wrong. The liberals were "not even wrong")!

- Atheism is not a claim but rather, the absence of a claim—or a claim that there is no claim to make.
- Atheism is not a stand but rather, the absence of a stand—or a stand that there is no stand to take.
- Atheism is not a philosophy but rather, the absence of a philosophy—or the philosophy that there is no philosophy to hold.

Atheism is a non-statement masquerading as a statement and is therefore doubly false. To ask that which is absent to form an opinion on that which is present, or to even tell the difference between absence and presence, is futile!

Atheism appears to have lost its standing, at least in theory, at this point.

How will it turn out, when considered in practical terms?

I have never, ever seen an individual live as if there were neither evil nor good. Even in the debate room, there is an aggressive effort to win the argument, showing that there is a difference between winning and losing. It can be tested by just flinging a slander in hurtful, sarcastic language and observing how ready and willing the recipients are to breathe fire down your neck! They really shouldn't, if there is no evil! The idea that everything is neutral is completely impractical. Nobody has ever lived it out.

The final portion of the "declaration" has the words "nothing but." This phrase is stating an absolute. It can tolerate no exception whatsoever. Even if one exception is found, it will prove the claim false. Here, the phrase refers to blindness, pitilessness, and indifference. Will it stand simple observation?

Is blindness universal? Whether it is taken literally or as a metaphor, the claimant's own statement proves it false, for sight would have to be absolutely necessary to pen those words. Sight, and not blindness, is universal.

Is complete lack of compassion in our existence? What then is it that flows out of a mother toward her infant? What has driven a thousand projects, overcoming seemingly insurmountable obstacles, to bring food, water, education, and hope to the under-privileged in a hundred countries? Probably those who sit in swivel chairs in air-conditioned luxury have never seen what I have. Compassion and pity mark our experiences at every level. One can deny it only on a piece of paper that is disconnected from the book of our existence.

Is everyone indifferent to everything, at all times? Please! For heaven's sake! This is tunnel vision that is refusing to lift its gaze to the object to be seen. Consideration, thoughtfulness, and attention pervade and soak through the lives of the masses on earth. How far away from reality can we possibly hope to run?

Need it be said? "Nothing but blind, pitiless indifference" is, on all counts, a fabrication. The whole of the atheistic declaration cannot stand theoretical or practical scrutiny, and therefore, is false!

We are left with the first three options. Of these, the first and third are not debated. The second—the claim that there is a loving God—requires attention.

Addressing the Contradiction

The contradiction arose because of the claim that there was something supernatural—God—and that He was wise, loving, and powerful.

We are, then, dealing with wisdom, love, and power that do not belong to our realm of existence but to that of God. What could be the explanations, looking at it from the angle of the supernatural? We cannot be certain. The most we can attain to is a conjecture, and then feel for the reasonableness in it.

1. God permitted evil in His wisdom, and He had a good reason for it. He withheld the explanations from us, also for a good reason, one of which was that we could not be able to understand or appreciate them just yet (it would lead to even more confusion at this time).

2. God's love is true. True love cannot but allow complete freedom of choice. Since love is a free expression, that which is coerced or automated is not love at all. This choice, therefore, could also be misused or abused. Humanity misused it and brought into its own existence, principles that were self-destructive. This has allowed evil to express itself in pain, suffering, and other baleful results.

3. Evil is only temporary. God will ultimately wipe it away permanently. The time is not yet. But when it comes, and when He destroys evil completely, it will be a display of His omnipotence.

4. Eternity/infinity is a concept within which there is a description of heaven, and the possibility that God will give to us, in that existence, that which will compensate us a million times over. The enjoyment and bliss will be so great as to dwarf all the troubles and sufferings we now experience.

   This will sound far-fetched, like "pie in the sky" today, and must be necessarily so, because the descriptions are coming from *God's* realm to us.

The presence of evil could suggest that God's love expressed itself in true form to give us our freedom of choice. The final destruction of evil would show that He is all-powerful. Once evil is exterminated, He will provide heaven, which is grand enough to more than compensate us for every suffering we will have ever experienced. The contradiction today is only apparent. The ultimate state will show the perfect harmony between the love and power of God.

If God does not exist, there is no possible explanation for good or evil, and actually, no explanation is needed. If God exists, the explanations are consistent with His character and have the potential to lift us from aimlessness and despair to a vibrant, purposeful, and hopeful life!

A correct and deep understanding of atheism has been a confessed cause of suicide, even without pain and suffering thrown in to add to it. A correct and deep understanding of the hope God offers has amazingly turned around would-be suicides—in the midst of their suffering, pain, and despair— into benevolent, happy, constructive members of their community. These are not carefully crafted theoretical claims but real-life experiences that form empirical and therefore, undeniable evidence regarding the effects of theism.

Conclusion

Evil, pain, and suffering are all around us. While it is very distressing, the argument that it is evidence for atheism is quite unfounded, especially because there is a lot of good within our experiences too. The presence of good, suggesting the presence of God, is the defining feature of our existence, despite the presence of evil.

Atheism has no explanation for the presence of good or evil, and in trying to avoid the difficulty in supplying a reason, it makes statements which expose its stand. This stand, on examination, is found to be untenable, impractical, and false. Thus, it appears that there are really no consistent, full-time atheists!

Theism does not explain the conflict between the love and power of God in terms of our present existence alone. It appeals to its basic claim regarding the existence of the supernatural and attempts to reconcile the conflict in the light of eternal values. Taking the perspective of eternity, it is possible that there is complete harmony between an almighty, loving God and the presence of evil today.

Atheism does not alleviate the pain and suffering in the world one iota. On the contrary, it could add to the despair and depression already prevalent.

Theism, by itself, also does not alleviate pain and suffering but can bring in hope and purpose, which are able to lift our spirits and make us happy, constructive neighbors, despite experiencing evil, which is the common lot of humanity.

So theism, even if ultimately wrong, produces a quality of life here on earth that appears superior to the hopelessness and despair that atheism must produce, if ultimately correct!

With the ultimate unknown, and with only the present evidence to go by, I would more than readily opt for theism!

Appendix B: Ultimate Design Versus Aimlessness

Abbreviations used:

EV = Evolutionism, Naturalism, Atheism

CR = Creationism, Intelligent Design, Theism

A raging controversy between EV and CR has been going on for generations now, with name-calling, barbs, and taunts all thrown in for good measure. Because neither side wants to relent, some attempt to marry the two concepts. When it comes to certain scientific observations, there could perhaps be a remote possibility, but on the level of their fundamental claims, they are worlds apart. William Provine, of Cornell University—a prominent figure in a prestigious think tank called CSICP (Committee for the Scientific Investigation of the Claims of the Paranormal)—described the attempt as "intellectually dishonest."

Susan Haack, also of the CSICP, stated, **"I agree with Provine that the hope of reconciliation is ill-founded"** (*Skeptical Inquirer,* March/April, 2004). I tend to agree with them. Each side piles up a mountain of evidence for itself and then points to the deficiencies of the other, claiming that the issue has been settled. Each side ends its arguments with flourish and finality, saying, "What's left to argue about?" Consider here two statements from the opposing camps, each very confident about its own claims:

> **"The universe we observe has *precisely* the properties we should expect if there is at bottom, no design, no purpose, no evil, no good, nothing but blind, pitiless indifference"** (Richard Dawkins, Oxford Biologist in Science, 277, 1997, emphasis mine).

> **"All the seemingly arbitrary and unrelated constants in physics have one strange thing in common—these are *precisely* the values you need if you want to have a universe capable of producing life"** (Patrick Glynn, in *God: The Evidence,* emphasis mine).

How can "precise" scientific information lead to such mutually exclusive positions? The answer is really quite simple, at this early stage in our discussion. Both EV and CR are not primarily based on observable/scientific facts but on diametrically opposing world views and philosophies regarding cosmic origins and human existence. True, both have appealed to scientific facts, but they have interpreted them by their own undergirding principles.

So no matter what the staggering discoveries in science, CR will explain them with, "God made it that way." And no matter how "mysterious" or "miraculous" the event or phenomenon, EV will retort with, "Just wait—it will eventually be explained in naturalistic terms." Both can stand whatever argument is brought to them. Both cannot be shown to be false, even if they are. This can happen only in a make-believe world of fiction. But since they are mutually exclusive, reason demands that we accept only one, and in doing so, we will have discarded the other. Let's try to clarify the bases.

EV—Every phenomenon is natural. Nothing is super-natural.

CR—God preexists everything and created everything—all phenomena.

EV—Unexplained events should be called "paranormal," because when all the information is in and science has conquered its last frontier, they will all be explained by natural laws alone.

CR—God is without beginning, endless, eternal, and infinite. He miraculously created the universe and all life. He holds all laws in His hands, so can produce supernatural phenomena.

EV—The only question is one of time. Wait—all the answers will come eventually—and only in naturalistic terms.

CR—The only question is one of recognition. God is at work in a million places—so just acknowledge the truth of the matter.

The debate continues, century after century, because one can start with either proposition and build a fair case. The other reason is that it is impossible to directly evaluate and thus prove or disprove either claim. EV appeals to the future, which is clearly outside our grasp. CR appeals to the realm of God, to which we also are unable to attain. The only way to decisively settle the controversy is to get to that ultimate state, and from that vantage point, make a pronouncement. But that is plainly impossible.

We are left with only our own experience and knowledge, within our present sphere of existence. The piles of evidence are not yet sufficient—the questions linger. Therefore, I think that, for today, the debate should include an abstract grappling of the philosophies themselves, on the level of reason and common sense. Yes, extrapolating from our present knowledge in an attempt to explain the unknown is fraught with uncertainties, yet we have no option but to try, because (a) the options are mutually exclusive and we cannot but live under one or the other, and (b) the choice is not between "black and white" or "right and wrong" but between "the most reasonable and the least reasonable."

(It is worth reminding ourselves that a "good" option could turn out "bad," if we chose the second best while the best was available. Conversely, an apparently "bad" option [because of the questions that remain] could turn out "good," if the alternative were to be worse—absurd and untenable.)

The issue at hand that we are going to consider is:

If EV is correct, our existence and that of the universe originated by random chance and is ultimately purposeless, aimless, and useless.

If CR is correct, our existence was conceived in the mind of God and designed with an ultimate purpose and destiny.

After reflecting on these for many hours and over many months, I wrote out the points of discussion which follow.

1. Scientists acknowledge that the farthest back one can go, theoretically, is to one ten million, trillion, trillion trillionth of a second—but not to "zero" time. Alan Rex Sandage, at one time known as the greatest observational cosmologist in the world, said that science had taken us to the First Event, but cannot take us farther back, to the First Cause (Strobel, *The Case for a Creator*, p. 70). Therefore, even singularity and the Big Bang are post facto. Scientific explanations should not pretend to reach back to "zero" time. Let's look at one attempted explanation.

> **"Singularity has no 'around' around it. There is no space for it to occupy, no place for it to be.... There is no past for it to emerge from. And so, from nothing, our universe begins"** (Bill Bryson, *A Short History of Nearly Everything*, p. 10).

Does this sound like a scientific explanation? Not to me. It appears nothing more than simple guesswork, a mental groping in the dark, and should be permitted to be dismissed by anyone, without a second thought.

> There exists **"... the tendency to rescue scientific appearances by evading the mythological point of our science"** (Matt Cartmill, Duke University anthropologist, quoted in Jonathan Wells, *Icons of Evolution*, p. 222).

EV cannot claim to have an answer. Nothingness is not an answer. Rather, it is absence of information, whose equivalent is, "I don't know." Therefore, the theory cannot make a statement regarding either purpose or non-purpose, because it lacks a basis.

CR claims to have an answer. God, a Mind, an Intelligence, is the First Cause. This theory is in a position to postulate that there is ultimate purpose and design. However wrong it might turn out to be, CR has something to offer as an ultimate theory.

2. If the ultimate state is an aimless one, the EV theory is proposing three phases/levels:

a. Origin—Random, aimless

b. Our existence—Abounding in aims and purposes

c. Ultimate state—Random, aimless

The focus is on the second phase—our existence. From the cry of a baby for milk, to the painstakingly precise work in a space-lab, our activities are shot through with purpose. We perform thousands of purposeful acts. Our whole lives revolve around the notion that only purposeful lives can be a blessing to society. Even an insane individual believes his thoughts and actions to be reasonable. Why would anyone think of proposing any other type of existence?

For the theory to have some credibility, there should be an explanation for its proposal. We live immensely purposeful lives (b). Nothing in observational information points in any other direction. No basis whatsoever seems to exist for suggesting (a) or (c).

The next question would be regarding the mechanics involved. How did the change occur, from the aimless existence of inanimate matter, to the purpose seen in human life? Further, what factors will change our "little" aims in life to make them, at the final count, utterly futile? The answers will have to be arbitrary. It fails as a viable theory, because no explanation can be given for the change from an aimless origin to solid, present purpose, and then back to ultimate aimlessness.

The CR theory is consistent. Purpose existed to begin with; there is purpose today; therefore, the ultimate state should be a purposeful one. The extrapolation from our present circumstance to possible origins and on to the ultimate reality, is a reasonable one.

3. EV claims that, given time and a series of discoveries, we will reach a point of being able to explain everything in terms of natural laws alone.

Every fresh bit of information generates its own set of questions that then require more discoveries in order to provide answers. In other words, we did not even know the questions we needed to ask, prior to the new discovery.

"It seems the more that is known, the more acute the puzzles get" (Nicholas Wade, in *The New York Times,* June 2000). The dictum: The more the facts, the more the questions. Or, the more the known, the more the unknown. Therefore, the mysteries and miracles that need explanations are only going to increase in number and magnitude. We are not gaining ground. With each new fact, the hope of explaining everything is receding farther and farther away. If that is the direction in which we are headed, the EV claim is only wishful thinking and is not based on reality.

But just suppose we will come to that point—then let's imagine the process. The more we know, the more we know we don't. This will continue to the critical point where we reach the state of the maximum unknown—the maximum number of unanswered questions. Then, to reach the point of maximum knowledge, the threshold will have to be crossed at that point of maximum ignorance. Suddenly, presto! What we know will equal all that can possibly be known. No questions will remain. But what factor will have caused this crossing over? It cannot be added information, because that would bring in added questions. It cannot be a deletion of information, because that would deplete the reservoir of knowledge. In reality, there is no such factor. The crossing over is an impossibility. If that state were ever to be reached, we would have gained the status of "omniscience"—all-knowledge, the state of God—the very state that is being denied. The theory cannot sustain itself on reason or logic—it is a fantasy.

Some scientists are willing to confess to it. Steven Weinberg (Nobel Laureate) appropriately entitled his book, *Dreams of a Final Theory: The Search for the Fundamental Laws of Nature.* Weinberg is said to have referred to Karl Popper (whom he called the dean of modern philosophies of science), who suggested that there may not be an ultimate theory for physics. A rival possibility is that such knowledge may simply be beyond us (Bryson, in *A Short History of Nearly Everything,* p. 168).

EV will have to concede that mysteries will remain; and as long as they do, naturalism will be under question. It could remain as a fanciful possibility, but there would be no basis for converting it into a scientific claim.

4. Randomness, aimlessness, purposelessness, disorder, and chaos do not need an explanation. Indeed, the reason they are described as such is because there is no explanation. If a reason or aim could be ascribed, that event/phenomenon would no longer be random, chaotic, or aimless.

EV claims that ultimately, there will be an explanation to everything. This should include our existence. It also claims that ultimately, everything is purposeless and aimless, including our existence. But there cannot be an explanation—which should include aim, reason, or purpose—to that which is aimless and purposeless. So either the ultimate state has an explanation with an aim and purpose, OR, it is random and aimless, with no explanation possible and none needed. It cannot be both.

If the first, it is a pointer to an Intelligent Mind—God.

If the second, it overthrows naturalism, which claimed to provide all the explanations. The only alternative to that is CR—God, with ultimate purpose!

5. One way EV discredits ultimate design is to question the existence of God. CR uses the logic that random chance alone will not account for the existence of life. Sir Fred Hoyle, an eminent British astronomer, likened the chances to that of a Boeing 747 coming together by itself. EV turned the argument around and, pointing to the "Ultimate Boeing 747" as meaning God, asked what the chances were of God coming together spontaneously.

The question, on reflection, appears to be a deliberate approach to slip-slide away, rather than to enter into a healthy, fair debate.

a. The question is based on EV's idea that God was created/formed at some point. But that is exactly the bone of contention. CR would never call this created entity God. The argument is like shooting arrows and then painting the targets around them—a bull's eye at every attempt!

b. The question presupposes that there is universal agreement on this point. Nothing could be farther from the truth. This is like demanding to be acknowledged the winner, as a prerequisite for the debate.

c. To go over the fence and change the claims of the opponent to suit yourself, and then shoot down the touched-up, tailored proposition, is both unfair and pitiful.

   CR is clear and unequivocal that God is without beginning and without end, that He dwells in infinity, is omniscient, and can hear and respond to millions of people simultaneously. It would amount to creating a "straw man" if any of these attributes were changed. The correct, fair approach is to show the claim wrong, not to change the claim itself. One way would be to show that there is no such thing as omniscience. But naturalism would falter and fall, if omniscience is not invoked.

"When we finally reach the long-hoped-for Theory of *Everything*, we shall see..." (Richard Dawkins, *The God Delusion* (London: Bantam Press, 2006), p. 144, emphasis supplied.

This appeal is to the state of all knowledge. The information at that point could explain how to listen to and respond to millions of people simultaneously. But the impossibility of that was used to deny the existence of God. The objection removed, back to God we go! The claim regarding the "Ultimate Boeing 747" is that it did not need to come together—that it always was. This claim has been tampered with, because, it appears, it cannot and has not been overthrown.

> **"For the scientist who has lived by his faith in the power of reason, the story ends like a bad dream. He has scaled the mountains of ignorance; he is about to conquer the highest peak; as he pulls himself over the final rock, he is greeted by a band of theologians who have been sitting there for centuries"** (Robert Jastrow, astronomer, *God and the Astronomers* (New York: Norton, 1978), p. 116.

6. To think of a state in which thought was non-existent, is impossible. The moment you think of it, thought has entered. Similarly, you cannot imagine a scene where no imagination exists. For the moment you have imagined it, imagination has arrived. If you remove thought and imagination from the scene, you cannot imagine or think of it.

Those who describe the origins of the universe in natural terms imagine the whole story before writing it down. In that history, life and thought would have to appear at some point. But the writer was there in thought and imagination, even before these came to be. That would be a contradiction. One way to reconcile this would be to acknowledge that life and thought always existed, even before singularity.

> **"Where are these laws written into that void? What 'tells' the void that it is pregnant with a possible universe. It would seem that even the void is subject to law, a logic that exists prior to space and time."** Heinz Pagel, *Perfect Symmetry: The Search for the Beginning of Time* (New York: Simon & Schuster), p. 243.

Logic requires an active, intelligent mind. A potential is necessary, prior to the actual. For example, the potential for movement should exist before running can take place. What is the potential, the *a priori,* for life and thought? Nothing appears as possibilities except life and thought themselves. Since we live and think today, it is reasonable to assume that life and thought have always existed, even at or before singularity.

7. EV states that once life got going, natural selection sprang into place and took over the process which has resulted in the complex life we observe on earth. The only "miracle" required was that of life. After that, the laws of nature supervened, and evolution became a **"cumulative one-way street to improvement"** (Dawkins, *The God Delusion,* p. 141).

A "one-way street" is not a description of aimlessness but rather, denotes direction and therefore purpose and aim. If these were the hallmarks of life right from the word *go,* why should anyone attempt to delete them from a description of the ultimate state and leave it totally aimless and purposeless? The idea is jarring, because it is so arbitrary. It also is unsatisfying, because there is no explanation that can account for such a suggestion. Science has always respected the "data-to-inference" type of thinking. Where and what are the data for this hypothesis? More in line with science would be to infer that the final, core state of the universe and our existence has purpose and reason, because these permeated the universe from its birth till today.

8. Millions of dollars have gone into SETI (Search for Extraterrestrial Intelligence), because it is just possible that we are not alone in the universe.

What will distinguish an intelligible signal from the crackle and buzz of plain old static? A design would need to be detectable in the signal. Static has no discernible pattern to it. Whereas, if there was maybe a code that could be interpreted by laws and rules, the inference would be unmistakable. If that code, received from outer space at different locations around the world, was decoded and found to contain the equivalent of a whole set of the *Encyclopaedia Britannica,* it would amount to incontrovertible evidence of life and intelligence out there. Language and communication, as a given, require life, intelligence, and volition.

What if that language and communication were found in "inner space," such as in the DNA of the 75 trillion cells in one human body alone? DNA is an intricately coiled ribbon, about six feet in length, packed into a space a thousand times smaller than the dot at the end of this sentence. It contains enough precisely coded information to fill a whole set of the *Encyclopaedia Britannica* and is not just passive information scribbled on a page. Rather, it's a set of complex, non-negotiable, active commands, which, if disobeyed, have dire, if not lethal, consequences. These orders are received, processed, and sent out at lightning speed beyond the nuclear boundaries, via specific messengers, and affect every part of the body. The process includes coding, decoding, editing, proofreading, adding, deleting, qualifying, and quantifying messages. The product is a precision molecule that is manufactured, packaged, addressed, and transported for a specific function, to a specific location, where it is unpacked, prepared, and fitted into the mechanism there. No human can produce and insert such a mind-boggling apparatus into the nuclei of cells. We must concede the inherent presence of language and commands; of submission and obedience to those commands; and therefore, of purposes and aims. If this is found in the nuclei of trillions of cells; if those same features are found in the community-lives of hundreds of millions of us *homo sapiens;* if we are now ardently hoping to find it among the clusters of gigantic galaxies spread over billions of light years of space; then we have effectively encompassed the universe as our horizon. We have acknowledged that there is ultimate purpose everywhere. What will we gain by denying it?

9. EV claims that the data referred to by CR to describe design can be interpreted differently. According to Richard Dawkins, if we "raised our consciousness," we would be able to see that the design being claimed is only imaginary and is only "apparent" and an "illusion." In reality, there is no design.

What is the difference between "apparent" and "real" design? It cannot be in the pattern itself; otherwise, there would be universal agreement on the point. To just say "Raise your consciousness" is more like a chant or mantra, which could be an illusion itself. The only way to label them as "apparent" and not real is to prove the designer as nonexistent. No other way appears available. And those claiming "real" design must face a similar consideration. The moment "design" is challenged by the claim of "apparent design," it should not be touted as fact till the ultimate is shown to be real.

So, are both the same? They might appear to be deadlocked. But they are not. EV's statement can stand only on reaching the level, and proving the non-existence, of the designer. It is not a deduction based on observation or reason. CR's statement is based on real observations of design, from which a reasonable deduction was made. How can anyone inspect the motherboard of a computer and the inside of a space shuttle and claim that there was only "apparent" design?

On the other hand, when there is apparent *chaos*, there could be design hidden in there. When passing a cornfield, it may appear as if the plants are scattered at random, till a particular point is reached where the design and order in the rows and rows of neatly planted corn become clear. All the other angles showed chaos, although order was always present.

Similarly, once even a single design or pattern is established, the possibility of ultimate design in the face of apparent disorder should be entertained. The terms have to be reversed. It is *disorder* and *randomness* that are "apparent" and therefore an "illusion."

10. If the ultimate state is purposeless and aimless, no purpose or aim at any other level or circumstance should matter. Even trying to prove everything aimless is in itself an aimless endeavor. Whether anyone accepts or rejects aimlessness, or accepts or rejects purpose, should make no difference, finally. Can there be true purpose in proving or even claiming that everything is ultimately purposeless?

If so, then everything is not purposeless. If not, why do it? For even if it were done just to kill boredom, it would still demonstrate purpose. The proposition is self-defeating.

The fact is, those who advocate it exhibit great purpose and aim in trying to explain its validity. They want to be known for their excellence in reasoning it out—and in that very effort, they establish the over-riding place of that which they are so keen to deny.

I sense that they do not really believe it but prefer to state it that way, for an ulterior motive, aim, or purpose!

11. Ultimate aimlessness means that at the origin of the universe and of life, no purpose existed regarding anything. What then is the explanation for the first organism "choosing" to live and not die? At least the next generation should have ceased to exist. Dying would not have needed a choice at that primeval stage; living would have required it. The sheer number of living organisms that not only exist but adapt and thrive today should convince us that choice was integral to the survival of life. Choice indicates, first, a grasp of some degree of knowledge, however rudimentary—and second, the ability to weigh it out before making a decision. Aimlessness cannot discern the essential difference between existing and not existing, so cannot form the basis of a choice. In fact, to choose is to stop being aimless. Aimlessness cannot account for the trillions of organisms that abound and flourish on earth. The most reasonable theory should involve life, thought, and volition, even prior to the origins of matter and life.

12. The principle governing EV theories is: **"Given infinite time or infinite opportunities, anything is possible."** Richard Dawkins, *The Blind Watchmaker* (New York: Norton & Company, Inc., 1996), p. 139. The statement is scientifically flawed, because time is finite. But that aside, I wonder if they really believed it; for if they did, the "anything" should have included "God" and "Creation." But these are strictly excluded, without bothering to address the inconsistency.

The statement is too simplistic and elementary to actually portray anything.

With it, neither side wins, although they are opposing and mutually exclusive claims. We are left in the position of the proverbial ass that died of starvation when faced with two equidistant and equally desirable bales of hay, because it could not give a single reason for preferring one bale over the other, so went to neither!

Here's my story of "Anything Is Possible":

" The elephant is gone!" rang out the shout in the camp. We all went running to where the elephants were kept. The large enclosure, where the bull elephant used to be chained, was empty. The bamboo fence facing the jungle was broken, the tall grass and little plants looked stamped upon, and there was the semblance of large footprints leading off into the jungle.

A buzz was heard, as everyone prepared for the search. But I, being the chief in the camp, stopped them. "It's no use. Let's give up."

"We can get him, if we go right away."

"Where will you go looking for him?"

"We'll follow the footprints—they are but a few minutes old."

"He didn't go off into the jungle. We'll never find him."

"Why not?"

"Because a baby ant swallowed him up."

"Baby ant? Don't be silly!"

"I'm not being silly. I did notice a baby ant yesterday, scouting around on that bamboo fence with both its antennae pointing straight to the elephant—and with a very hungry look in its eyes."

"Come off it! That's ridiculous. It's impossible!"

"No, it's not. Here's my explanation. Matter is made up of atoms and molecules which are mostly space. If the electrons would stop their endless spinning and settle down together with the protons and neutrons, all that excess space could be eliminated. The difference would be enormous.

"The matter making up that ponderous creature could easily get into the stomach of a baby ant. In fact, a dozen or more could fit in.

"There now, I've produced as scientific an explanation as any. None of you can disprove my theory. None of you can give a more 'scientific' explanation. The question is settled. No more talk. Expedition disbanded!"

A rousing round of applause broke out, at the exceptional wisdom and leadership I had displayed. Everyone turned to go back to their workstations. But one little girl still had a puzzled look on her face. She was the same one who had earlier been in the streets lined with crowds waiting to see the emperor's new clothes, and who had exclaimed, "But Dad, the emperor has no clothes on!" End of story.

Of course, anything is possible. With a broken fence and visible footprints staring us in the face, we are still allowed the freedom to cling to a scientific "baby ant" explanation. But it will sound like an "old-fashioned folk tale" being told as a "bedtime story" by an "outright crackpot"!

At the level of simple reason and common sense, I think the gavel should be brought down on the side of Ultimate Design and therefore, Ultimate Purpose.

Appendix C: Relativism

Relativism versus Absolute Truth. What do these terms mean?

Absolute Truth: This refers to statements we call facts that are true/ valid for all people, in all places, and at all times. They could also be called universal truths. Also, they are independent of observation and belief, meaning that whether or not they are observed, whether or not they are believed, they still remain facts and will always be so. All facts are not absolute. Relative truth does exist and has practical application, but only when connected to some absolute truth. For example, Mt. Everest, at 29,028 ft., is the tallest peak in the world, while Kanchenjunga is relatively lower in height. This is true, despite people's personal opinions and even if it is completely disbelieved.

Relativism: The claim here is that there is no such thing as absolute truth in any sphere of life. A statement can be true only for certain people, in limited places, and at specific times. Such a statement is dependent on a variety of factors and conditions, including observation and belief. The mind is what gives form and quality. The mind is where reality is created, and each mind can produce its own "truth" or "fact" from what is observed. For example, the statement that Mt. Everest is the tallest, is only a questionable claim. This report has to be believed and trusted for it to become fact. And even then, it could be wrong. Therefore, all so-called facts are only relatively true and there is no absolute truth at all.

"There is no objective standard by which truth may be determined so that truth varies with individuals and circumstances." David Trueblood, *Philosophy of Religion* (New York: Harper & Row, 1957), p. 348.

"It will become clear that there is only one principle that can be defended under all circumstances and in all stages of human development. It is the principle: Anything goes" (Paul Feyerabend, quoted in McDowell, *New Evidence That Demands a Verdict,* p. 617).

"The postmodern world view affirms that this relativity extends beyond our perceptions of truth to its essence: there is no absolute truth; rather, truth is relative to the community in which we participate." Stanley Grenz, *Primer on Postmodernism* (Grand Rapids, MI: William B. Eerdmans Publishing Company, 1996), p. 8.

"Foundationalism, the idea that knowledge can be erected on some sort of bedrock of indubitable first principles, has had to be abandoned" (Millard Erickson, quoted in McDowell, *New Evidence That Demands a Verdict,* p. 617).

No question existed that Relativism was taking a stand completely against Absolute Truth. The gap was unbridgeable—one or the other. I had to check it out.

A. The word *absolute* pictured something rigid, fixed, and exclusive, while *relative* pictured something flexible, easy, and inclusive. But on reflection, it was *Relativism* that was making the exclusive claim—only it was correct and valid, while Absolute Truth was actually non-existent. The claim was that *all* so-called facts were only relatively true. This exclusive claim seemed to go against its own grain.

B. To the question, "Is relativism valid universally?" the answer has to be in the affirmative. In other words, Relativism was valid for all people, at all times, and in all places. An absolute truth! Asking this in another way, "Is Relativism the only truth?" the answer again has to be in the positive, and in that very answer, it has once again established an absolute truth! Relativism has no option but to contradict itself.

C. Relativism claims that a statement can only be relatively true. By that same token, it can also be false. If the statement is regarding Relativism, then it (Relativism) is also false, so cannot claim to be universally true, as in the previous point.

D. If Relativism is relatively true as well as relatively false, it depends on another factor, say, my choice, to make it one or the other. If I choose it (Relativism) to be false every time, it will be absolutely false!

E. To decide whether it is true or false, there has to be a factor, say A, that makes it one or the other. But factor A itself is only relatively true and therefore, is relatively false. We will have to consult factor B to decide whether A has to be taken as true or false. But factor B is no better than factor A, since it too is only relatively true. We will need factor C, then factor D, and on and on, ad infinitum! Each step will go farther and farther away from the original question, that now has no hope of ever being answered. This is called "infinite regression"—we keep backing away from the questions, without answering them.

Relativism does not allow answers to be formed or accepted. Therefore, its own answers to questions have no validity. It thus chops the branch on which it is perched.

F. Only when a statement is relatively false can its antithesis, Absolute Truth, be valid. But Absolute Truth dominates completely by its very nature of being absolute.

It cannot be valid for only a portion of the time. Can Absolute Truth be wrong regarding the same point, at some of the other times? The absurdity becomes apparent.

G. In this concept, words could have exact opposite meanings.

"Love" could be "hate," in a relative sense; "come" could relatively be "go"; "in" relatively "out"; "pass" relatively "fail," and so on. Language would be stripped of its ability to communicate, and we might as well be living on different planets, or, as Ravi Zacharias says, "in a madhouse"!

H. The word *relative* suggests a relationship. To be practical and real, one entity has to be set or fixed. For example, where would our place of rendezvous be if we agreed to meet 100 yards to the left of the train, which itself was traveling from Los Angeles to New York at a hundred miles an hour? Relativism is just that practical.

I. In trying to qualify truth and falsehood, Relativism blurs the boundaries suggesting that they might be at different points on the same spectrum. But they are poles apart, in essence. Falsehood can masquerade as truth and not vice versa. One can deceive only by falsehood, not by truth. Truth lies within boundaries, all else is false—this cannot be reversed. The two are made of different "substances."

Otherwise, it would be like going to buy a gold bracelet and demanding that it be made of cast iron. What would the composition of the final product be?

J. Relativism must address the other side of the coin, which is "falsehood." To be consistent with its stand (which amounts to an oxymoron, because Relativism, by definition, cannot be consistent), it must claim that falsehood is so only relatively, and is therefore also relatively true. Falsehood could be true! Then, an oath in a court of law could run like this: "I swear to state falsehood, the whole of falsehood, and nothing but falsehood. But, Honorable Judge, not to worry—my words will all be relatively true." What a travesty that would be!

K. If we agree that there are opposing concepts, we have confessed to the existence of both. For example, to state that something is heavy is to agree that something is also light. If every load on earth were the same weight, there would not be any reason to call one "heavy" or "light." So to claim that truth is relative is to confess that there is truth that is absolute. If even one absolute truth is around, Relativism goes out the window.

L. If everything is relatively true, then everything is relatively false.

M. Relativism is not an axiom—it is a deduction. And if so, it has to be based on principles of reason and logic. It can be communicated by language only if the words adhere to standard meanings at all times. Relativism, therefore, relies completely on absolute values, yet denies those very values.

N. The quote from Paul Feyerabend claimed: "Anything goes." This is the same as saying "Everything is acceptable." If that is what is really being said, then Absolute truth should also be acceptable, because it has to be included in the "everything" or "anything." The statement has defeated itself.

O. What have some others said?

a) "So, it looks like any apparent suggestion of relativism is either self-defeating or else is not a real assertion, but something more like an empty slogan." Michael Jubien, *Contemporary Metaphysics* (Malden, MA: Blackwell Publishers, 1997), p. 89.

b) Norman Geisler is said to have stated: **"Most relativists believe that relativism is absolutely true and that everyone should be a relativist. Therein lies the destructive nature of relativism. The relativist stands on the pinnacle of an absolute truth and wants to relativize everything else."** And again: **"So if truth were relative, then an impossible would be actual."**

c) "Subjectivism is not an 'ism,' not a philosophy. It does not rise to the level of deserving our attention or refutation. Its claim is l ke 'I itch' not 'I know'" (Peter Kreeft, *Handbook of Christian Apologetics,* 1994, p. 372).

d) "Postmodernism's rejection of rational objectivity is self-defeating. It either denies the plausibility of its own position or it presumes the reliability of reason and objectivity of truth." Dennis McCallum, *The Death of Truth* (Minneapolis: Bethany House Publishers, 1996), p. 53.

e) "To assert that 'the truth is that there is no truth' is both self-defeating and arbitrary. For if this statement is true, it is not true, since there is no truth" (William Craig, quoted in McDowell, *New Evidence,* p. 620).

f) "To say 'It's true that nothing is true' is intrinsically meaningless nonsense. The very statement—'There is no absolute truth'—is an absolute truth." Gene Veith, *Postmodern Times* (Wheaton, IL: Crossway Books, 1994), p. 16.

g) "We have no compelling reason to accept the theory. We can simply dismiss it as a creative work of extremely cynical people" (McCallum, *The Death of Truth,* p. 53).

h) "The laws of logic must apply to reality; else we may as well be living in a madhouse" (Ravi Zacharias, *Can Man Live Without God?* p. 11).

i) "A mood can be a dangerous state of mind, because it can crush reason.... But that is precisely what I believe postmodernism best represents—a mood" (Ravi Zacharias, *Jesus Among Other Gods,* p. vii).

By way of summary, here's an anecdote:

"A friend of mine told me that when Christian apologist and author Ravi Zacharias visited Columbus to speak at Ohio State University, his hosts took him to visit the Wexner Center for the Arts. The Wexner Center is a citadel of postmodern architecture. It has stairways leading nowhere, columns that come down but never touch the floor, beams and galleries going everywhere, and a crazy-looking exposed girder system over most of the outside. Like most of postmodernism, it defies every cannon of common sense and every law of rationality.

"Zacharias looked at the building and cocked his head. With a grin he asked, 'I wonder if they used the same techniques when they laid the foundation?'

"His point is very good. It's one thing to declare independence from reality when building a monument. It's another thing when we

have to come into contact with the real world" (McCallum, in *The Real Issue,* quoted in McDowell, *New Evidence,* p. 620).

Relativism was not a philosophy and not an "ism." Full of contradictions and phantom-like as to its real nature, it was more like a "slogan" or a "mood." It would be suicidal to base any of my major decisions on it. So it was out for the count.

Appendix D: Pluralism

In trying to clarify the idea of Pluralism, I drew a diagram like the one below:

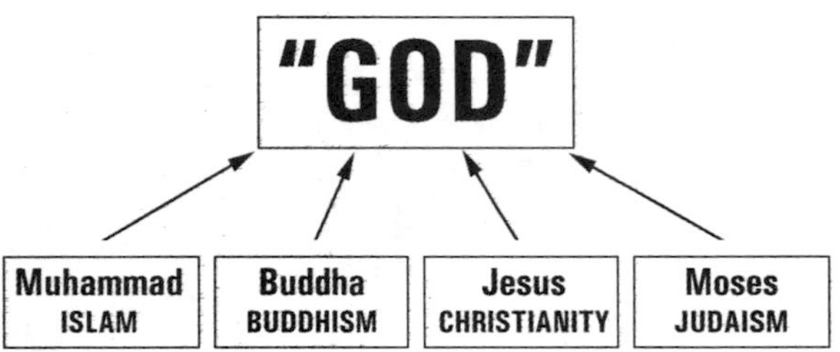

On seeing it, a friend exclaimed, "That's exactly what I believe!" "And why so?" I asked.

"Well, I think that when anybody worships or prays to or thinks about 'God', the name may be different, but that Supreme Being is the same."

"Then you do not claim to hold to any religion?"

"Actually, I'm a Buddhist. But I believe everyone's religion, be it Hinduism, Christianity, or Islam, leads to the same Ultimate Being, just as in your drawing. I can't see how anyone can claim this or that to be the only correct one."

"Does Buddhist literature ever state that Brahma, Vishnu, or others, along with Buddha, lead to this Ultimate Being?"

"Hmmm—I guess not."

I found this idea of "all roads leading to Rome" to be espoused by the majority. Sometimes, it was not an open claim, just a lingering suspicion in the back of the mind, even among those professing their faith strongly.

> **"When Jews or Muslims, for example, praise God as Creator of the world, it is obvious that they are referring to the same Being. We may assume that they are intending to worship the one Creator God that we also serve.... If people in Ghana speak of a transcendent God ... how can anyone conclude otherwise than that they intend to acknowledge the true God as we do?**
>
> **"Of course Buddhism is not Christianity and does not try to be. But how does one come away after encountering Buddhism and deny**

that it is in touch with God in its way?" Clark H. Pinnock, quoted in Ramesh Richard, *The Population of Heaven* (Chicago, IL: Moody Press, 1994), p. 81.

"God is in the world—but Buddha, Jesus, Muhammad are in their little closets, and we should thank them but never return to them." W. E. Hocking, *Living Religions and a World Faith* (New York, MacMillan, 1940), p. 231.

"To understand God is to listen. Listen to Jesus and Muhammad and Buddha, but don't get caught up in the names. Listen beyond them; listen to God's breath"—a Zen saying, quoted in *God's Breath*, John Miller and Aaron Kenedi, eds. (New York: Marlowe & Company, 2000), back cover.

"Pluralism — recognizes not only the existence of other religions but their intrinsic equal values." Timothy George, *Is the Father of Jesus the God of Muhammad?* (Grand Rapids, MI: Zondervan), p. 128.

Whenever I asked if this was found in their written literature, there was hesitancy first, then a slow acknowledgment that it was not there. So I went to the various scriptures to see what really was there.

HINDUISM

"I am the goal, the upholder, the master, the witness, the home, the shelter and the most dear friend. I am the creation and the annihilation, the basis of *everything*, the resting place and the eternal seed" (Bhagavad-Gita, 9:18).

"Let there be one scripture...for the whole world—Bhagavad-gita;Let there be *one God* for the whole world—Sri Krishna: one hymn, one mantra, one prayer—the chanting of his name" (Introduction to the Bhagavad-Gita).

ISLAM

"Allah! There is *no God but He*—The Living, The Self-subsisting, Supporter of all—His are all things in the heavens and on earth-- His throne doth extend over the earth—He is the Most High, The Supreme" (The Quran, 2:255).

"Verily I am Allah; There is *no God but I*" (The Quran, 20:14).

BUDDHISM

"This Lord is truly the Arhat, fully enlightened, perfect in his knowledge and conduct, well-gone, world-knower, *unsurpassed*, leader of men to be tamed, teacher of gods and men, the Buddha, the Lord" (Conze, *Buddhist Scriptures*).

JUDAISM

"For thus saith the Lord, who created the heavens, who is God, who formed the earth.... I am the Lord and *there is no other*" (Isaiah 45:18).

"I have sworn by Myself; the word has gone out of my mouth in righteousness, and shall not return, that to Me *every knee* shall bow" (Isaiah 45:23).

CHRISTIANITY

"For there is *no other name* under heaven, given among men by which we must be saved" (Acts 4:12).

"I am the Way, the Truth and the Life. *No one* comes to the Father except through Me" (John 11:24).

These statements were unequivocal, sharp, and clear. No ambiguity need be entertained. No, I did not find in any of the writings the sanction that the other religions were a good, equal alternative.

"In a broad sense all religious traditions are exclusivist, inasmuch as they maintain their central affirmations to be true." Ramesh Richard, *The Population of Heaven* (Chicago: Moody Press, 1994), p. 73.

"The exclusive claim has long been assumed on all hands. Even Hinduism which with some justice prides itself on a hospitable stance is, from that angle just as rejectionist of Semitic instincts as it sees them to be" (K. Cragg, quoted in *The Population of Heaven,* p. 73).

"At the heart of every religion is an uncompromising commitment to a particular way of defining who God is or is not and accordingly, of defining life's purpose.... Every religion at its core is exclusive." Ravi Zacharias, *Jesus Among Other Gods* (Nashville: Word Publishing Group, 2000), p. vii.

"What is truly arrogant is the postmodernist pluralism which, in

vain pursuit of a superficial tolerance, negotiates away the ultimate commitment by which any religion lives" (George, *Is the Father of Jesus the God of Muhammad?* p. 93).

"Agreement...cannot be made without substantial compromise of core beliefs." Paul Marshall, et al., *Islam at the Crossroads* (Grand Rapids: Baker House Company, 2002), p. 34.

A severe clash occurred between the sacred writings and the claims of Pluralism. Both could not be valid; in fact, they were mutually exclusive. I would have to examine Pluralism.

A. Exclusivism came "ready made," inherent in the written codes. Pluralism, on the other hand, was a development. It had to be built up from scratch and could claim, as its basis, only opinions and suppositions from various individuals. And all they were trying to do was explain the writings.

   The problem was that the explanations were going contrary to the written claims.

B. To show necessity for change, evidence must be provided that the old was deficient, irrelevant, defunct, or false. But Pluralism could not claim to find irrelevancy or falsehood, yet say that they were all equally *valid* and *true*. To find anything to change would be to make Pluralism irrelevant. The need would be to fix that problem and not bring in Pluralism.

C. The claim of equality presupposes a universally acceptable reference point. If two people claimed to be the same weight, they should have gone to the same weighing machine. But there is no such reference point for religion. How can civilized society accept that voodooism and witchcraft and child sacrifice are equal to Buddhism or Islam or Christianity?

D. To replace anything, the authority over that jurisdiction has to be established. The religions themselves held independent authority within the religion and the body of believers, and they clearly claimed exclusivity. Pluralism had only a derived, second-hand one, if any, and therefore was not in a position to overturn any claim of the religions.

E. If Pluralism claimed to oppose only the principle of exclusivism and not the religions themselves, it would have to show evidence that the religions did not claim that position. But the writings were too clear—they were claiming exclusivity, so Pluralism was definitely challenging the religions, at least on that point. Pluralism was questioning the truth of their claims, yet saying that they were all true. You can't "have your cake and eat it"!

F. The religions claimed that their information came from a supernatural source and was brought to us humans accompanied by unusual, "miraculous" phenomena. This is what authenticated their status as superhuman. Nothing in Pluralism existed to match this. And it was only an opinion, with just that much weight to its claim.

G. The Zen saying already cited asked us to listen *to* the founders and also to listen *beyond* them. The problem arose when you really attempted that, because when you listened *to* them, they were unquestionably decided that you should never listen *beyond* them to anyone else. For example, if you listened *to* Muhammad, he would emphatically tell you not to listen *beyond* him. So we have a choice either to listen to them or beyond them. To do both is not possible. The Zen saying is not practical.

H. To be really serious in matters of eternal consequences, there should be a clear promise of rewards on compliance and an equally clear description of the consequences of non-compliance. Furthermore, since this would involve detailed, unerring judgments, the power and ability of that source would become extremely important questions. A claim should be available that no mistakes would be made—that the final judgments would be infallible. Pluralism had nothing to back itself on this point.

I. If even one religion claimed to be exclusively correct, then to leave them all as before, yet to say that they were all equal, would be to give them equal as well as exclusive status at one and the same time. This would not be a logical or practical stand. Either exclusivity or equality—but not both.

J. If we acknowledge that all religions lead to the same '"God" and retain the fact that this "God" gave each its exclusive standing, then this "God" could be called a liar—and a devious one, at that. Such a God presumably told the Hindus about their numerous deities, then struck down that whole concept with Muhammad's fiercely monotheistic declaration. This "God" would have reveled in this duplicity, pitting one against every other, creating strife and animosity down through the ages. The worst wars in history, after all, were "religious" wars! Pluralism has to own up to this concept of "God."

K. Proper names are a precise form of identification, and once given, society demands that we respect that identification as distinct. Of course, many people can have the same name, and one person can have many names, or aliases. Pluralism refers to this "God" with many names. The plea is that since there are many similarities, the reference is probably to the same Ultimate Being. But similarities are not as much the deciding factors as are differences. If we found 100,000 similarities between two complex organisms, would it make a difference if one's name were Adolf Hitler, and the other's was Mother Teresa? *Even one irreconcilable difference* will negate all the similarities to be found.

Allah is the proper NAME of God in Arabic. Jesus is the NAME given among men.

Aliases could be a possibility, but not once in the Bible is Allah an alias for Jehovah or Jesus, and not once in the Quran is Buddha or Vishnu an alias for Allah. Not once! With reference to the drawing at the beginning of this Appendix section, there is no "God" above Allah or Jesus or Brahma. Nobody has yet demonstrated the authority or the rationale for changing these names to a generic form.

L. To introduce and sustain Pluralism, the initial requirement is to go to the founders—Muhammad, Jesus, Moses, or others—and show them to be wrong, bigoted, and intolerant and compel them to change their declarations to suit your idea of truth. Whatever method is used, the attempt will end up in complete despair or in mutilating the religions to a point beyond recognition. All that will be left will be a heap of garbled, incoherent, meaningless utterances, for which you can give neither rhyme nor reason. Try it and see for yourself.

M. To follow all religions at the same time is not possible. One religion, or portions of different ones may be possible. So could an individual choose any part of any religion, at random, to make up a set of beliefs? But that would be forming a new religion, and this new one would take its place among the others, just as did the others before it. The round of questions would start all over again. Making circles is not a sign of progress.

Furthermore, a new "God" would be needed. But a "manufactured" God would have no inherent power or position—only that which the individual has seen fit to bestow. Who would be dominant—"God," or the individual?

N. The religions not only claimed exclusivity, they pointed to the drawbacks of others.

"The Buddha held that this belief in a permanent self or soul is one of the most deceitful delusions ever held by man" (Chen, *Buddhism, the Light of Asia,* p.44). He (Buddha) was referring to the core teaching of the Hindus.

"All who ever came before Me are thieves and robbers" (John 10:8). These are the words of Jesus.

They **"... are like a donkey laden with books. Wretched is the example of those who deny God's revelations"** (The Quran, 62:5).

This statement from the Quran refers to the Jews and Christians.

Statements such as these make it impossible for Pluralism to maintain the concept that they all are equally valid, good, and credible, and therefore, acceptable.

O. An illustration keeps making the rounds, whenever this topic comes up—the story, from the poem of John Godfrey Saxe, of the king's elephant that three blind men felt and described. One felt the tail and said the elephant was like a brush. The one whose arms circled the leg called it a tree. The one who played with the trunk pictured it as a pipe. So, in the religious world, each religion is but a part of the whole, and people are able to describe and advocate only portions of the actual whole. Nobody should ever claim that his or her statement is the only and last word on the subject.

It sounds good, until it is questioned. The three blind persons represent the whole of humanity. Then who is the king, and who is the story-teller? If they are not of this world, then what is their identity? How did the reporter know that there was a king and an elephant? If they are part of humanity, how did they escape the universal blindness, so as to be able to see the elephant and the other blind people? Both the king and the poet are actually non-existent. Therefore, any report is a fabricated one, or from just another blind person who cannot claim to have seen the elephant. The illustration lacks a fundamental basis.

More reasonable would be to opine that we all have tunnel vision and are able to appreciate only certain narrow, limited values. The brush, the tree, and the pipe are different entities, just as are the different religions, and each is claiming to be the truth. No basis exists for saying that they all ultimately belong to one identity—one generic religion.

P. Pluralism takes a cue from another common expression: "All roads lead to Rome." Thus the claim that all religions are only different paths to the same final destination. During the days of the Roman Empire, the roads did not start out in the periphery. They were built centrally first, and then went out in all directions. In other words, the destination came first and preceded the network of roads. This cannot be said of religious endeavors. Our starting point and the direction of progress is exactly the opposite. We have not reached the destination. And that brings us to the most crucial observation. Rome was established in the minds of people as real, concrete, and well known. Universal agreement prevailed regarding this reality. Once in Rome, one could observe the fact that all the roads were leading there. The various travelers coming in and going out could also vouch for it. The expression was valid only because of this. Without a real Rome—without real journeys to and from that real destination—there would be nothing to back the expression. Likewise, in the case of religions, this expression of Pluralism would be valid only if the destination had been actually reached from different paths, coming from different directions. But truth be told, there is no universal agreement regarding the destination. We cannot vouch for anything about it, let alone its relationship to every road. Then what is the basis of saying that these roads actually reach there? Can there be any other way of validating the claim? No, indeed there cannot! None of those who make the claim have been to the destination and back. Alas, then, the base, the foundation, is absent. The claim has lost touch with reality.

Pluralism is nothing more than wishful thinking. It is not found in the sacred writings, and the reasons for it do not stand scrutiny. As an honest inquirer, I must lay it aside and prefer the clear, exclusive claim of each religion.

Bibliography

Bibliography

_________The Bible, New King James Version, Nashville, TN: Thomas Nelson Inc., 1979, 1982.

_________The Quran, Translated by N. J. Dawood. New York: Penguin Books, 2000.

Armstrong, Karen. *Muhammad.* New York/San Francisco, HarperCollins Publishers, 1992.

Chen, K. K. S. *Buddhism, the Light of Asia.* Hauppage, NY: Barron's Educational Series, Inc., 1968.

Cohen, Abraham. *Every Man's Talmud.* New York: Schocken Books, 1975

Conze, Edward, trans. *Buddhist Scriptures.* New York: Penguin Books, 1959.

Green, Michael. *But Don't All Religions Lead to God?* Ada, MI: Baker Books, 2002.

McDowell, Josh. *The New Evidence That Demands a Verdict.* Nashville, TN: Thomas Nelson Publishers, 1999.

Muncaster, Ralph. *A Skeptic's Search for God.* Eugene, OR: Harvest House Publishers, 2002.

Prabhupada, Swami A. C. Bhaktivedanta. *Bhagavad-Gita As It Is.* Alachua, FL: Bhaktivedanta Book Trust, 1986.

Strobel, Lee. *The Case for a Creator.* Grand Rapids, MI: Zondervan, 2004.

Subramaniam, Kamala, trans. *Mahabharata.* Mumbai, India: Bharatiya Vidya Bhavan, 2004.

Wells, Jonathan. *Icons of Evolution.* Washington, D.C.: Regnery Publishing, 2000.

Zacharias, Ravi. *Jesus Among Other Gods.* Word Publishing Group, 2000.

For your personal copy of *Cross-Examination*, or for additional copies, contact your local Christian bookstore or mail your prepaid order ($14.99, plus $5.00 shipping and handling) to: **CAMPUS p.r.e.s.s.**, P. O. Box 2402, Ann Arbor, MI 48106, USA. Website: www.campus-press.org.